Recipes
from my
French
Kitchen

Allyson Gofton has been cooking for New Zealanders for nearly 30 years. She is known for her recipes and columns in magazines, television appearances, radio slots and many personal appearances in the name of charity. She has also written more than 20 cookbooks, including her bestselling series of books *Bake*, *Cook* and *Slow*, as well as the popular *Country Calendar Cookbook with Allyson Gofton* and her latest bestseller *Good Food Made Simple*.

To Jane & Jim,

With best wishes

Allyson G

Allyson Gofton

Recipes
from my
French
Kitchen

Contents

Map of Caixon

Cèpes

La grande villa

Ruine de
la tuilerie

Lamayou

Le pont

L'école

Monument
de la Résistance

Bascule

Mairie

Le moulin

L'église

Les Pyrénées

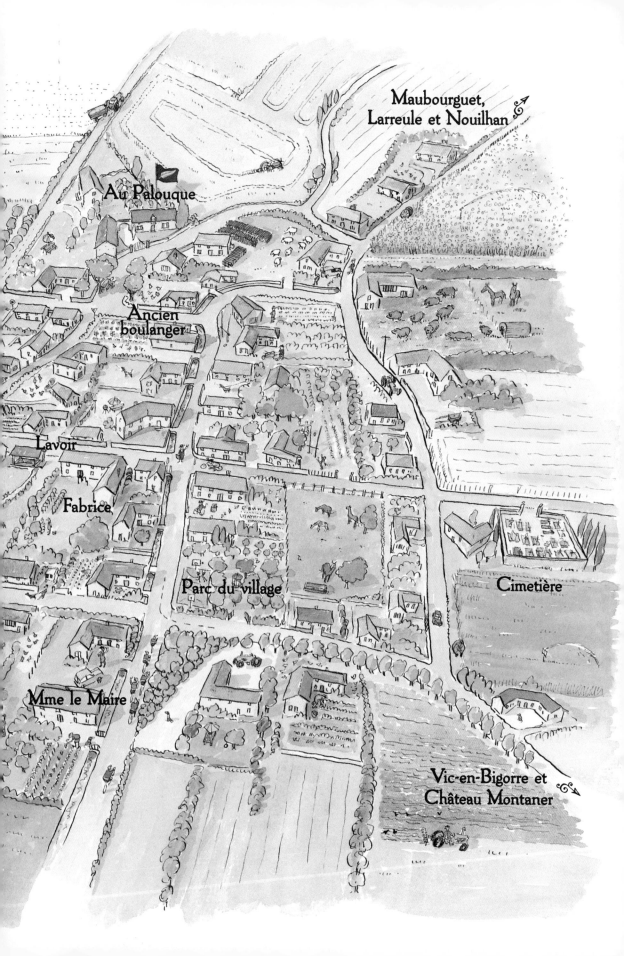

Maubourguet,
Larreule et Nouilhan

Au Palouque

Ancien
boulanger

Lavoir

Fabrice

Parc du village

Cimetière

Mme le Maire

Vic-en-Bigorre et
Château Montaner

Introduction

Life is full of beginnings and endings; it's what happens in between that makes the difference. For us the beginning was my husband Warwick's dream of living overseas for an extended period. Realising this dream became more urgent as he approached fifty, but by then the family included Jean-Luc (10) and Olive-Rose (5), replacing the original vision of a free-wheeling couple doing their own thing in some European paradise with a much more organised family adventure. Warwick thought it would be a good idea for the children to learn a foreign language through immersion, and we chose French.

Thus, in November 2012, the Gofton-Kiely family drove through the gates of the converted farmhouse of Au Palouque, Caixon (pronounced 'kay-song'), in southwest France, Department of the Hautes-Pyrénées, Region Midi-Pyrénées – read backblocks. The village – one of many – lies in the valley of the Adour River, which rises high in the snow-capped Pyrénées Mountains. The land around it is the plain before the mountains rise to the Spanish border, and is mostly given to growing wheat, maize for stock feed and vegetables, and grapes for Madiran wine. A flourishing artisan food industry is evident in the markets held in every village, but nevertheless this is an area of high unemployment and most working-age residents travel to the nearby town of Tarbes or even further afield to earn a living. The result is a village of largely older people, although Caixon does have the small primary school that Olive-Rose attended, with Jean-Luc going to school in the neighbouring village of Larreule. Many of the houses stand empty for most of the year, their owners returning only for holidays. Some have been 'rescued' by retired British immigrants, many of whom operate accommodation options. Even more of the old farmhouses, manors and even châteaux are slowly crumbling back into the earth from which they seem to grow.

The nearest town, Tarbes, is 30 kilometres away, the somewhat larger Pau is an hour's drive and the city of Toulouse over two hours, so Caixon and its neighbours are part of a declining community. Smaller shops have closed – there were none in our village, the advent of a supermarket hastening their demise – and only the over-forties do their shopping in the traditional markets that circulate around the villages over the week.

Caixon was ideal for my city-raised children to become free-range, to be free to cycle around streets mercifully free of traffic, to play and walk unfettered. Importantly, the venture also gave me the opportunity to accept a contract to write, beyond recipes, a book about our experiences, encapsulating the seasons, customs, people and foods of the Hautes-Pyrénées – a dream come true for me. For Warwick, who had taken to cycling in mid-life, it was the perfect place from which to pedal, including over stretches of the Tour de France routes.

We arrived in the dark at Au Palouque, and it was not until the next day that I saw our new home from the outside. Standing on a carpet of frost, kids squealing with delight,

I began to feel our adventure was really happening. It didn't take long to create a Kiwi home-away-from-home in this century-old farmhouse with its weathered riverstone walls that attested to many additions and alterations down the years.

Downstairs was one big room with a huge fireplace – around which we huddled before roaring blazes in winter – and the dining table. This room opened out to a courtyard on one side and the front garden with its cherry trees on another. My office and a bathroom were off the third side, and the kitchen off the fourth. The bedrooms were upstairs, with uneven, creaky floorboards and heavy-beamed low ceilings. In the handkerchief-size upstairs bathroom, you didn't dare drop the soap in the shower as you had to get out of the shower to pick it up! The septic-tank loo had a sign that said '6 sheets per sitting', a concept totally alien to small children.

The kitchen led through to a huge storeroom/cellar with the shell of a massive bread oven once used by the whole village, now long disused. In the kitchen, the one small barred window let in little daylight, augmented by a few eco lightbulbs sitting precariously in a rustic wrought-iron chandelier. Festoons of extension cables that would give a health and safety inspector nightmares attested to a lack of power points around the house. Indeed, the entire electrical system was more than somewhat limited: having more than two appliances operating at once caused it to give up altogether!

A small, round, green and white tile-topped table made from an old wheel served as a workbench and breakfast table, although its height suggested that its creator might have been related to a Hobbit! It was definitely a one-person kitchen when it came to meal preparation and couldn't be more of a contrast to my own kitchen at home.

Behind the house, an extensive grassy area boasted numerous fruit trees and a neglected veggie patch crouched miserably under a mountain of branch trimmings, waiting for some hard work to restore it to productivity. The front of the house, with its generous lawn, proved an ideal place for the kids to play, and there were the bones for me to work some gardening magic. It was love at first sight.

In Caixon, I became just another anonymous international immigrant, however temporary, a situation not aided by my total lack of knowledge of French. It was a complete change from being recognised so often wherever I went! I was, for the first time, a full-time wife and mother who planned her days around school, housework, cooking and nurturing.

Of course, it wasn't all plain sailing and, if I'm honest, I was very close to throwing in the towel in the first couple of months, especially as Warwick flew back to Auckland on business, leaving me with the children two weeks in to this strange new environment.

I cannot begin to describe the sense of isolation that assailed me. It was winter, and the village and its surrounding countryside were a picture in monochrome . . . stark, black trees against a lowering grey sky, fallow paddocks and no people. Well, that was when you could see anything but the frequent dense walls of fog!

In winter, the villagers retreat into their thick-walled homes, close the shutters and light the fire, only emerging for necessary shopping, church and the like. I saw other mothers when I took the children to school, but there was little connection, partly because of the language difficulty and partly because they didn't hang around to chat. I was desperately lonely and homesick and, without the few English-speaking friends I had started to make, I could have fallen into a deep depression.

Fear of being branded a quitter kept me going, so I buckled down and determined to make the best of things – even if that was through recurring tears. Helping me pick up my bundle were the managers of our *petite maison* (small house), Au Palouque. Quintessential British Francophiles Graham and Irene Clarke, who would later become close friends, encouraged me to be bold and see beyond the closed shutters and reserved ways of the locals. Taking my hand, they helped me learn that it was better to stumble and fall with my French than not to try.

Spring came on the dot, 1 March. The village shutters were thrown open and the sun began to shine as the trees donned their spring foliage and came back to life. I got stuck into the garden to make a vegetable patch, planted lavender from the blue wrought-iron gates to the front door and threw open my own windows to let in the light and warmth. Life began to hold great promise.

As the weather improved, activities in the villages and surrounding countryside also blossomed until there was almost too much going on, and we couldn't get to see or participate in everything. All such activities are community-based, as is life in this area, and the sense of community is very strong. I found myself with a renewed enthusiasm for finding out as much as I could. Life was still largely bounded by the neighbouring villages, school and markets, but there was plenty for me to discover and learn about the food of this region, often still called Gascony by the locals. It has had a turbulent history and now suffers from the more recent phenomenon of urban drift, no different to our own country, where the young no longer want or are able to stay on the family farm and have moved to the city. Change is constant, although its pace varies.

We went to Caixon to live, learn and eventually fall in love. This is our family's story, peppered with recipes and anecdotes from a largely unknown area of France, an area of exceptional beauty, captivating locals, deep-rooted customs and love of traditional foods.

For all the effort, the tears and tantrums, our adventure became a year of unforgettable family memories.

PAGE 8: *Me outside Au Palouque, our home in Caixon.*

THESE PAGES, CLOCKWISE FROM TOP LEFT: *Jean-Luc and Olive-Rose at our gate; our French home; solid-oak hand-built doors with heavy iron locks featured on all out-houses; Vic-en-Bigorre market; springtime in Caixon.*

Caixon

Neatly tucked between oak- and chestnut-wooded *crêtes* (ridges) on a small, rich agricultural plain in the wide Bigorre Valley, Caixon, a centuries-old village of a dozen or so laneways, is just a dot on the map, en route neither to nor from anything or anywhere significant. For travellers on the D935 – a main road from Bordeaux to the ski fields of the Pyrénées – not one signpost indicates the village's existence. Maybe that's why it has remained so untouched and beautiful.

Caixon is characteristic of the villages of the northern tip of the Hautes-Pyrénées. Behind high moss-clad walls and splendid wrought-iron gates stand substantial stone-walled villas, farmhouses and barns, relics of the days when wealth poured into Caixon from the *tuileries* (tile factories) located at the western end of the village, long abandoned to nature to bury.

The commune of Caixon has its own Mayor for its 377 inhabitants. It is one of over 36,000 communes in France, but more locally it joins with 28 neighbouring communes to form the Communauté de Communes Vic-Montaner, of which the main town is Vic-en-Bigorre. This is a system in which the communes work together to achieve established goals.

Caixon's history is a tapestry of empires and eras. It was known in Roman times, and its name in Latin translates as the 'domain of Cassius', an ancient Roman family name. During the Hundred Years' War from 1337 to 1453 (yes, it was longer!), the village comprised a castle, a mill, a church and a church enclosure, the remnants of which form the nucleus of the present village. Caixon became home to the Bishops of Tarbes until the Wars of Religion in the mid-1500s wreaked devastation in the area, including Caixon and the church. The church, rebuilt in the seventeenth and eighteenth centuries with its baroque-style bell tower and three ornately carved and gilded wooden altars, is now a classified historic church of the area.

In 1814, towards the end of the Peninsular War, Caixon was in the path of Napoleon's army, which was in retreat from a hiding by the Anglo-Portuguese troops of the Duke of Wellington, after the battle of Orthez north of Pau. The Napoleonic troops were singularly disliked, as they pillaged en route, while Wellington's forces were respected for paying for what they needed – or took!

The Franco years saw the support of Spanish refugees in the region. There was the decimation of a generation in the Great War, and more tragic loss in the Second World War when this area, which was occupied by the Germans, was active in the Resistance movement; Caixon has memorials to four young men who were shot by the retreating Nazis. Just along the road from Au Palouque, a large villa – under which the river once ran when it was the mill – had been a nightclub for German officers. Those times are still raw here and not spoken of.

The immediate area around Caixon was once swamp, but it was drained long ago by skilled Dutch engineers, whose labours revealed stones for building and clay for tiles. The name of our farmhouse, Au Palouque, means 'swampy marshland'.

Buoyed by income from the tileworks until the 1950s, Caixon boasted cafés, a tavern, two weekly markets, a fruit and vegetable store and even horse racing. Today these buildings are home to families, not commerce. With its delightful school, it is a village for both young and old. The fit and able young commute to bigger towns for work. The elderly, in blue-check, cover-all working aprons or with beret-crowned heads, and bent forms often supported by hand-carved walking sticks, embody a way of life of peaceful privacy and a generous kindred spirit – the key to Caixon's uniqueness.

décembre

The ploughed paddocks, denuded
trees, buckled and aged tiled roofs,
large wrought-iron gates – everything we
saw was blanketed in white.

THE GLORIOUS, FRESH, AUTUMNAL DAYS that greeted our arrival in mid-November continued until early December and then ended abruptly.

Thick, white frost resembling snow greeted us one morning, along with an equally impressive minus 5°C on the thermometer, and the mercury kept on dropping for the rest of the week.

The ploughed paddocks, denuded trees, buckled and aged tiled roofs, large wrought-iron gates – everything we saw as we headed to Jean-Luc's school was blanketed in white, like a scene from *The Snow Queen*. To add to the enchantment, three deer darted out in front of us and across the frozen paddocks to disappear into the forest, with a backdrop of the mighty Pyrénées. It was lovely to watch the children's delight in nature's white beauty.

Warwick returned to New Zealand early in the month. The loss of company and the solitary village life that accompanied the frozen weather were in stark contrast to the people-filled house that we had left back in Auckland, and loneliness crept up on us.

Hurdles that would normally have been easily cleared assumed much bigger proportions. Small bruises and cuts, usually fixed by comforting words, now required counselling and intensive nursing. As well, the primitive power system in the house often gave up the ghost through overloading, leaving me crawling under thorn-spiked branches in an unknown pitch-black garden trying to find the switch box to remedy things. Murphy saw to it that this always occurred at dinnertime – and when our one and only torch was not in its rightful place!

Worst of all was an unexpected storm of tears and tantrums. Gone was the euphoria of being the interesting, new kids at the school and in a rush came 'I hate it here; take us home'. I was unprepared for the tempestuous outbursts; in the happiness of the first few weeks at school, I had begun to think we were going to be immune from this sort of upset.

For Jean-Luc at 10, with no French and at the age of dawning self-awareness, the hurdle was higher than for Olive-Rose, who was at school with other new entrants. Jean-Luc's world collapsed and he wilted under the overload of new and unfamiliar surroundings and systems, and I had to collect a very upset child from school on more than one occasion.

Things settled down somewhat in time for Warwick's return just prior to Christmas, although we could have done without my crashing the car into the entrance barrier to the airport carpark. Once they were over the shock, the children told all and sundry about their near miss, and it was not long before calls came from teachers and villagers to check on our well-being; concern and kindness poured in from our new neighbours.

Dealing with the insurance claim the next day in the main town of Tarbes would have been funny if we'd been in the right mood. We knew it would take a while to sort out, but were completely taken aback when noon struck and we were ushered out of the insurance office and told to come back after 2 p.m.! It was lunchtime and nothing, but nothing, comes between a Frenchman and his four-course lunch. Well, if you can't beat them, join them, so we repaired to a café where, thanks to my lack of French food language, poor Warwick lunched off pickled herrings in dill sour cream, followed by *steak haché de boeuf*, an unseasoned minced patty served *au bleu* or raw. For a time, I was not popular!

By the time that drama was behind us, we were ready to concentrate on the festive season. It was so different without the usual stresses of exams, end-of-year school events, work deadlines to meet before the annual summer shutdown, and break-up parties. There was no mad rush for presents, no pre-Christmas traffic chaos, no fretting over the menu, no family squabbles over hosting the big day; none of the stress we usually associate with December and Christmas.

As real Christmas trees did not appear until a week before the twenty-fifth, we made our own. Gusty autumn winds had brought down branches and twigs, and each night after school we collected a load for kindling. Long branches painted red, white and silver, perched in a milk can and decorated with paper Santas, crêpe paper, tinsel and cellophane snowflakes made a fine Christmas tree.

Santa found his way down the chimney, despite some concern that he would not know where to find us, and after the predictable squeals of delight over presents, the kids joined me in the kitchen to get the festive meal underway. There was no turkey or ham this year, and not being game enough to try duck, the meat of the area, on the kids yet, we opted for a treat of roast New Zealand lamb, which I had found in the local supermarket, with all the trimmings.

A Christmas pudding, carried all the way from Tasmania via New Zealand, was dessert, and it was all washed down with a bottle of delicious French bubbles. For me the table decorations were most special. With wet weather and children indoors on the days before Christmas, we had used pages of A4 paper to make our table runner and table mats using felt tips, cut-out decorations, glittering sprinkles and whatever else we could find to add special touches.

In the afternoon, a number of local youngsters found us playing rugby in the front yard and joined in for a replay of the Rugby World Cup, Caixon-style. Sadly, the Kiwis lost the replay; mothers do not make good props!

On Boxing Day, all went back to normal; it is not a public holiday here. I spent the rest of December in the garden, digging the compost into the vegetable plot before leaving it to sleep under frost for early spring planting, and indulging in late mornings and early nights by the fire, much like every other family in our village. Nothing would happen in our sleepy part of France until the school doors opened again in early January.

PAGE *18, CLOCKWISE FROM TOP LEFT: Gâteau à la Broche (see page 282) on a festive home-made table runner; Christmas baubles on a neighbour's gate; the river Échez at Larreule.* THIS PAGE, CLOCKWISE FROM TOP LEFT: *Table decorations made by the children for our first Christmas at Au Palouque; candle holders were in short supply, so I reverted to the classic wine-bottle style for decoration; winter berries blossomed on our aged stone walls.*

Les Marchés de Noël

With only basic shops in the surrounding villages, we turned to *les Marchés de Noël* to source our gifts. Christmas markets are held in every small village, some run by the equivalent of our Parent Teachers Associations; others are larger and run by the village itself.

Local artisans fill stalls with hand-made creations: paintings, carved wooden toys, special foodstuffs like quince paste, glacé fruits, nougat (cut in a wedge from a truckle weighing about 5 kilograms!), woven rugs, pot plants and more. Each purchase was wrapped with attention to detail. Jean-Luc and Olive-Rose were in kid heaven hunting the stalls for family gifts, searching for the best ways to spend their five Euros on each other.

Our local Saturday market at Vic-en-Bigorre, our nearest large village, bulged at the seams in the two weeks before Christmas. Local bands took centre stage and played up-beat Banda music to cheer on the season. Fundraising groups set up *crêperies* (crêpe stands) on trestle tables where dozens of cooks tossed crêpes for hours. Sprinkled with caster sugar or lavished with Nutella, two over-sized crêpes cost a bargain one euro.

Each stall had a queue of dedicated followers waiting to buy meat, foie gras, duck, chicken, fish, shellfish (oysters sold in boxes of two or three dozen and *petite* to *grande* in size), cheeses, breads and traditional gâteaux, glacé fruits, marzipan-stuffed dates and nougat, fresh fruit and vegetables, flowers and more. Never before had we seen live turkeys being inspected before the fatal chop, sampled roasted chestnuts straight from the pan, indulged in so many fruit pastes, nougats or honeys. For Jean-Luc and Olive-Rose the bustle, din and chaos was like playing a live role in a Disneyland Christmas movie, and the entertainment was free!

Amandes
Pistaches
Noisettes

Christmas Celebrations

Village decorations were simple and subdued. Coloured flashing lights have not made it to Caixon, although there were the most delightful rope-ladder-climbing Santas hanging from farmhouse windows, lampposts, barn doors and fences. The unruly winter winds had tangled many of them, turning the old gents upside down, strangled and swinging in the breeze.

However, beyond the extreme adventure Santas, Caixon and other nearby villages kept their decorations very low-key. Branches from fir trees, tied with ribbon and trimmed with hand-made notes and winter flowers, were tied to the large and often ornate wrought-iron gates that protect many homes from the street. An occasional Christmas tree peeped through lace-curtain-veiled stone- or red-brick-edged windows.

Most villages have a local choir, and their multi-cultural make-up of French, British, Dutch and other European nationalities ensures that the Christmas carol repertoire is eclectic. We attended carols at the eleventh-century Church of Saint Martin in nearby Maubourguet; the kids were wrapped in blankets to ward off the cold at a chilly three degrees. Like all events, it started at 9 p.m.; both kids fell asleep during the singing, so Warwick and I could enjoy mulled wine and Gâteau des Rois in the old church after carols. Originally part of a Benedictine monastery, Saint Martin is on the pilgrimage route to Santiago de Compostela.

On Christmas Eve, again bundled against the chill, we attended midnight mass at Saint Martin in Vic-en-Bigorre. The exterior of this fifteenth-century church, resembling a crossword map with its mix of stone, brick, concrete and other materials, tells a tale of old beginnings, additions and repaired ruins. Inside it is ornately painted in a palette of faded sky blue, aged burgundy and cream. Spiritual depictions of Jesus and his followers embellished with layers of gilt stare forlornly down on the modern-day congregation.

Jean-Luc had boldly said, 'Yes' when he was asked to join the crew of altar boys, and since services pretty much follow the same order as English ones, his lack of French was no hindrance. This was his first midnight mass, held in candlelight and with great solemnity. Each member of the congregation, from sleepy, cherry-faced child to stern-looking parent and frail, elderly *grand-mère* (grandmother), held a long, slender, tapered white candle, and all these little flames combined to reflect brightly off the ancient gilded religious figures, illuminating this grand old church with flickering light.

There was much chatter as families caught up with each other, but as the bell tolled the last chime on the eleventh hour, Father Thierry-Joseph began his formal walk to the altar and silence descended. Jean-Luc drew the short straw, placed right behind the deacon who was in fine form, swinging the highly perfumed over-

filled thurible with great gusto; Jean-Luc had to duck and dive to avoid a coughing fit from the incense propelled over the congregation.

Mulled wine and fruit-laden sweet bread were on offer after the service and even though we spoke no French, we were swept up to join the celebrations. The clock struck midnight; it was Christmas Day and this service was a special start to our French *jour de Noël*.

Le Maire et la Mairie

Whether large like Paris with its population of over two million, or small like our village, Caixon, with 377 inhabitants inside 8.55 square kilometres, in France a team of councillors governs all communities, from which a Mayor is chosen to be the figurehead and representative of the village. There are more than 36,000 semi-autonomous communes with an average population of 380! Very little happens without the Mayor's permission or knowledge.

It has been this way since the French Revolution, and for many it is a way of life that maintains a micro-local identity of which they are incredibly proud and, in some instances, parochially so. However, with the population more mobile today, together with the rural exodus, many communes have had to join into *communautés de communes* (see page 14) to share resources and avoid duplicating services.

Caixon's *Mairie* (town hall) was built in the mid-1800s. Like many village town halls it is adjacent to the school, the running of which is a key responsibility, and near the church; these three buildings are the cornerstones of every village.

For newcomers, a formal introduction to the *Maire* (Mayor) is both required and appropriate, and meeting our Mayor, Madame Vignaux, was the first thing we did on arrival. In a country with formal manners and strict protocol, the importance of presenting yourself appropriately to the Mayor is not to be underestimated.

We nervously fronted up to what, months later, transpired to be a meeting with *Fawlty Towers* connotations! To start with, you never say 'I wish to introduce myself.' You must say 'I wish to present myself.' The former, we later learned, has an explicit sexual implication! Unwittingly, I had not known that the French word for kiss had two meanings. To cap off the farce, I got my *tu* and *vous* round the wrong way and treated Madame Vignaux as a long-lost friend of many years' standing! Thus, we revealed total ignorance of the formal codes of French etiquette, doubtless leaving the Mayor bemused at our lack of manners, not to mention paucity of French language skills!

It was hardly the best of starts, especially as we needed permission from the Mayor for Olive-Rose to attend Caixon *École Maternelle* (junior primary school), and for her to propose to the Mayor of Larreule, the neighbouring commune of 381 inhabitants and 10.4 kilometres in area, that Jean-Luc be accepted into Larreule *École Élémentaire* (primary school). Most importantly, we required a formal statement, complete with wax seal and signature, for proof of domicile in her village for our visas. Thank goodness Madame Vignaux, who subsequently became a friend, was accepting of her newly arrived *citoyens* (citizens).

Pumpkin and Chestnut Velouté

Smooth, creamy sauces or soups prepared from a roux base (butter and flour) with chicken or veal stock and finished with a liaison of cream and egg yolks are classically called a velouté. It's French for velvet or velvety, and it so perfectly describes what the texture should be – a gentle savoury cream that slips smoothly over the tongue; divine when properly prepared. The restaurants in our area always began their winter menus with a velouté soup, although many were more a purée of legumes finished with cream – no different to home. Pumpkin was undoubtedly the most popular, although my favourite, which I have tried to recreate faithfully here, from an *auberge* (inn or hostel) in Montesquiou, came richly thickened with chestnut purée.

Prep time: 15 minutes   Cooking time: 30–40 minutes   Serves: 8

1 onion, peeled and diced (white onion is best)
1 clove garlic, crushed and peeled
50 grams butter
5–6 cups chicken stock (home-made is best)
750 grams–1 kilogram pumpkin, peeled, deseeded and diced
250 grams canned or bottled whole chestnuts (do not use sweetened chestnut purée)
1 cup cream
2 egg yolks

In a large saucepan, cook the onion and garlic very gently in the butter over a low heat until they have softened. Do not allow the onion or garlic to burn.

Add the stock and pumpkin and simmer gently with the lid on until the pumpkin is so soft it is falling to pieces. Add the chestnuts and cook for a further 5 minutes until they have softened; this will make them easier to purée.

Carefully purée the hot soup – the finest texture will come using a stick blender – and then pour through a sieve. Return to a clean saucepan over a low heat.

Beat the cream and egg yolks together to make a very smooth mixture and slowly stir into the hot soup to give a smooth, velvety texture. Taste and season with salt and white pepper. Avoid black pepper if you can; it does tend to look like flies have walked all over your soup!

Serve with fresh, hot baguette. In France, bread comes without butter, but I so loved their gentle-flavoured butters that I always asked for some, often to the waiter's chagrin! Add a dollop of sour cream if wished, but avoid adding any garnish like herbs or croutons; these will overpower the delicate flavours of this creamy soup. If planning to freeze the soup, do so before adding the cream and egg yolks; add these when reheating.

Garbure

At the Vic-en-Bigorre market, Jean-Claude, owner of the *épicerie* (grocer's) stall, made me very welcome from our first day. It was cold and miserable, and Jean-Claude's beaming smile and patient manner helped me so much as I struggled with the weights and measures in French. At one end of his transportable stand he normally has buckets of olives, sun-dried tomatoes, preserved lemons, capers, anchovies, pickled capsicums and all the gourmet foods we associate with the Mediterranean. Tubs of crystallised fruits in every subdued hue reminded me of a paisley-patterned Liberty print, they were so pretty. Bins of rustic-toned legumes – chickpeas, Tarbais beans, split peas, fava beans – and rice – brown, ivory and claret-coloured Camargue rice – invited me in, and I bought bags full of dried goods to create wholesome winter soups and stews, beginning with the classic of the area, Garbure. Served throughout the Pyrénées, this winter cabbage soup can be broth-like or hearty and stew-like; a meal on its own.

Prep time: 30 minutes   Cooking time: 1½ hours   Serves: 8

1 cup haricot beans, soaked overnight in cold water
250 grams salted pork of any cut, fat included, skin removed if preferred
8–10 cups chicken stock (the locals use duck)
1 winter bouquet garni (see The French Pantry opposite)
1 large leek, cleaned, trimmed and sliced
1 onion, peeled and diced (brown onion is best)
2 waxy potatoes, peeled and diced (avoid starchy potatoes)
2 turnips or 1 swede, thickly peeled and chopped
2 carrots, peeled and sliced
4–6 cloves garlic, peeled and sliced
1–2 portions duck confit, fat and skin removed
¼ cabbage (Savoy will give the best texture)

Drain the beans well and pop into a large saucepan with the pork, which still has the fat on it – to remove it would be committing heresy here – stock and bouquet garni, and simmer away for 45 minutes or until the beans are about half cooked.

In a large and preferably wide frying-pan, cook the leek, onion, potato, turnip or swede, carrot and garlic in a seriously generous knob of butter until the vegetables have softened and begun to brown a little.

Add the vegetables to the beans, bring to a simmer and continue to cook for a further 20 minutes or so, or until the vegetables and beans are just about tender. At this point, add the duck to the soup and continue simmering for a few more minutes to finish cooking the beans and vegetables and allow the duck to heat through.

Remove the duck and pork from the soup and while both are cooling sufficiently to handle, chop the cabbage – don't fret too much about the uniformity or delicateness of the chopping, this is *paysan* or peasant fare – and add to the saucepan.

Shred the pork and duck and return to the saucepan. Once the cabbage has wilted, remove the bouquet garni and season. Add more stock if wished, and serve.

The French Pantry

For a more robust flavour in your southwestern French dishes, prepare a winter bouquet garni by wrapping several stalks of celery, thyme and parsley and a bay leaf between two long, dark-green leek leaves. Tie up with string. Dried thyme and bay leaves are perfectly acceptable.

Lamb Caixon-style

Getting a handle on buying cuts of meat took me some time and, for all my experience with meat cookery, I was lost when faced with whole sections of beef, some weighing as much as 30 kilograms and often still on the bone. In a desperate attempt to make a tender casserole, I turned to an old favourite – a shoulder of lamb that I could easily identify and cook with confidence, much to the delight of my children, who were not enjoying the shoe-leather-like casseroles I was turning out!

Prep time: 15 minutes   Cooking time: 3 hours   Serves: 6

4 carrots, peeled and diced
4 stalks celery, sliced (keep the leaves for garnishing)
1 leek, trimmed and sliced (avoid onion, it is too strong here)
½ cup green or brown lentils (use Puy lentils if you wish to indulge)
2 cloves garlic, crushed
1 bouquet garni (see page 31)
1 lamb shoulder on the bone (you need the bone for sweetness)
3–4 cups chicken stock (1–2 stock cubes and water will suffice)

Preheat the oven to 170°C and place the rack in the centre or just below.

Into a deep lasagne-style baking dish, scatter the carrot, celery, leek, lentils, garlic and bouquet garni. Sit the lamb shoulder on top, season well with pepper and salt and pour in 3 cups of the chicken stock around the side.

Cover with foil and bake in the preheated oven for 2½ hours. Remove the foil and continue to bake for a further 30 minutes or until the lamb is well browned and the meat is coming away from the bone. If you feel the lentils need a little more liquid, do add some.

Remove from the oven and, using two forks, pull the lamb from the bone and return to the lentil and vegetable mixture for serving.

I like to scatter freshly chopped celery leaves on top before serving. They add a fresh flavour and the lime-green colour of the leaves brightens the rustic nature of the dish more than parsley, which could be used if there are no celery leaves.

Serve with hot, crusty baguette, broken at the table into chunks to soak up all the delicious juices. Leftovers are just as tasty reheated the next day. If you have run out of juice, add some water when reheating.

Note to Cooks
I cooked this often in Caixon, sometimes changing the shoulder for a leg of lamb, but always cooking the meat until it fell off the bone. Cooking times were longer for a leg, about an extra 45–60 minutes.

The French Pantry

Puy lentils, grown in Le Puy-en-Velay region in the Haute-Loire, are slate-grey–green with an exceptional peppery flavour. Authentic Puy lentils are easily recognised as they will feature the French AOC – *Appellation d'Origine Contrôlée* (see page 224) – label and may also display the European Union's Protection Designation of Origin label. Look for these when buying. Puy lentils, as wonderful as they are, come at a price and you do not want to spend good money on a masquerading lentil! Excellent green lentils were grown in our area and came at half the price of the Puy; the choice is yours.

Pain d'Épice

Honey and spice cakes – of some description – are classically European; almost every country will have a version baked specially for the holy season. Both were once the domain of monks, who tended hives at their monasteries and utilised the therapeutic properties of spices, which were so extravagantly expensive they were only for the men of God or the wealthy. Thus monasteries became famous for creating these long-keeping, once-a-year celebration cakes or breads. A good Pain d'Épice needs time; like good wine, its making cannot be rushed. The batter must rest overnight before cooking; and afterwards the honey will only be able to weave its magic, creating a moist, mellow spiced cake, if allowed time to do so: a week or two, well wrapped in a cool place, is a must. Pain d'Épice was on sale everywhere in the weeks preceding Christmas and at varying prices, but I decided to have a crack at making my own for our first Christmas.

Prep time: 30 minutes   Standing time: overnight   Cooking time: 1½–2 hours   Makes: 1 large loaf

1½ cups whole milk
1 cup brown sugar (I prefer a mix of soft brown and muscovado; molasses is too strong)
500 grams honey (choose one with a robust flavour)
500 grams flour (if you can, use high-grade flour)
1 tablespoon Pain d'Épice spice mix (see The French Pantry overleaf)
1½ teaspoons baking soda (for a lighter *pain* use 2 teaspoons)
1 egg, beaten

In a saucepan, gently heat the milk and sugar over a low heat, stirring without boiling, until the sugar has dissolved. Remove from the heat and stir in the honey. If the milk boils, it will curdle; if this happens, don't fret – it will look messy but can still be used, although the finished texture may be denser.

Sift the flour and spice mix together in a bowl and make a well in the centre. Gradually pour in the milk and honey mixture, stirring until the batter is smooth. I like to use a sturdy large balloon whisk to do this, but a good old wooden spoon is just fine, although do make sure you have no lumps of flour. Cover and refrigerate overnight. This step is extremely important as it allows the starch granules in the flour to expand, which is essential in ensuring a moist, tender bread.

Preheat the oven to 120°C and set the rack just below the centre. Grease and line a large (26cm x 11cm or 8½–9-cup capacity) loaf tin. Alternatively, grease 16 x ½-cup capacity mini cake moulds.

Dissolve the baking soda in 1 tablespoon warm water and stir into the batter with the beaten egg. Pour into the prepared tin and cover with baking paper. If using moulds, place these on a baking tray – there is no need to cover them, as their cooking time will be much shorter.

Bake in the preheated oven for 45 minutes. Remove the paper and continue to cook for a further 1 hour or until a cake skewer inserted in the middle comes out clean. Small cakes will take about 1 hour.

Leave the bread to cool in the tin for 15 minutes, then turn out. Do not try to turn out the Pain d'Épice while it is still hot, as it will break into large pieces. When cold, wrap well in foil, leaving the lining paper on. Store in an airtight place for 1 week before venturing to slice. Any earlier and the flavour will not be mellow or the crumb moist. Best left for 2–3 weeks.

The French Pantry

There are as many versions of the spice for Pain d'Épice as there are shoe shops in France. I settled on the Albert Ménés brand, which uses cassia and mace. Cassia is the variety of cinnamon preferred in many European sweet breads and which has a much more vibrant flavour, while mace will always offer more to a dish when partnered with nutmeg – just as nature intended.

Mix 2 tablespoons of ground ginger with 1 tablespoon each of ground cassia, cinnamon, cloves, nutmeg, mace and cardamom and ½ tablespoon ground aniseed (or use ground star anise). Keep in an airtight container away from heat and light. Use to make spice biscuits. In summer, I added a large pinch to peaches when poaching them – scrumptious!

Rich Gâteau des Rois with Glacé Fruits

Throughout December, on Epiphany and until the Feast of the Baptism of the Lord, Gâteau des Rois (king cake) is sold everywhere. It can be flaky pastry sandwiching a rich almond filling. Or, confusingly, it may be a very light-textured egg-rich brioche, formed into a circle to represent a crown – the gâteau is also called *la couronne* (the crown) by some *boulangeries* (bakeries) – scented with orange blossom water and decorated with sugar crystals or glacé fruits. While both cakes are available throughout the year, during the festive season they come with a *fève* (porcelain bean or token) hiding in the dough, and a golden paper crown. When the gâteau is cut – a privilege usually accorded the youngest – whoever gets the bean in their piece is crowned king and wears the crown. A dried bean was used until the eighteenth century, when it was replaced by tiny porcelain figurines in the shape of the baby Jesus. After the Revolution the Phrygian cap became popular. In time, an industry sprang up and the *fèves du gâteau des rois* came in all manner of designs, such as the wise men, artisans and musicians. Liquor companies even used them as a promotion but, sadly, now they are more often plastic. While I was in Caixon I became a *fabophile* (collector of *fèves*) and now have more than I will ever require!

Prep time: about 4 hours   Cooking time: 25 minutes   Makes: 2

4 teaspoons dried yeast granules (use basic dried yeast here)
500 grams high grade flour, sifted
4 eggs at room temperature
½ cup sugar
¼ cup milk or water (approximately)
175 grams butter, softened but not melted
¾–1 cup chopped glacé fruits (I like to use cherries, orange peel, pears)
3 tablespoons orange blossom water (or use water scented with orange essence or extract)
1 tablespoon vanilla essence
1½ teaspoons salt

To decorate
chopped glacé angelica, cherries and orange peel
pastry sugar grains (see The French Pantry on page 40)

Into a large bowl put the yeast, ¼ cup of the flour, 1 egg, 1 teaspoon of the sugar and all the milk or water and beat to make a thick batter. Add a tad more milk or water if needed. Cover and set aside for about 30 minutes or until the batter froths and bubbles; this may take longer if you are working in a cold kitchen. This step is important to make sure the yeast has dissolved, as it will not do so once you move on with the recipe.

Beat the remaining eggs, setting 2 tablespoons of beaten egg aside for glazing the gâteau before cooking. Keep covered or the egg will form a skin.

Add the remaining beaten eggs, flour and sugar to the yeast mixture with the butter, glacé fruits, orange blossom water, vanilla essence and salt. Beat with one hand, while the other is holding the bowl, for 5 minutes. The mix should be thick, like a very stiff batter. It should not be the consistency of a bread dough that can be kneaded on a bench.

Cover and set aside for 2½–3 hours or until the dough has more than doubled in bulk. The slower the rising time, the more flavour the gâteau will have.

Turn out onto a floured board, divide in half and mould each half into a ball. Dust your fist and push it through the centre of each ball of dough to make a ring. Work the centre out to make a ring about 20cm in diameter – the centre hole should be about one-third the size of the ring.

Transfer to a baking-paper-lined tray. If using a token (*fève*), push one into each round from underneath.

Cover with a clean cloth and set aside for about 1 hour or until the dough has doubled in bulk. Repeat with the remaining dough.

Preheat the oven to 160°C. Once the dough has risen, brush with the beaten egg; decorate with glacé fruit and the sugar grains or, using scissors, make small cuts in the top of the dough.

Bake in the preheated oven for 25–30 minutes or until the dough is well risen and golden. Cool on a wire rack. Best served the day of making or the day after.

The French Pantry

Le sucre en grains – pastry sugar grains, also called pearl sugar – can be hard to find outside France. The sugar grains are about the size of a broken piece of short-grain rice. They are used in baking for decoration; they will not melt under heat. If you don't have sugar grains, decorate the gâteau with sliced glacé fruits.

Bread-maker Gâteau des Rois

Flavour this simple recipe with orange blossom water or vanilla, if wished.

Prep time: about 2 hours   Cooking time: 25 minutes   Makes: 1

2 tablespoons active yeast mixture (also called bread yeast mix)
1 tablespoon sugar
⅓ cup tepid water
50 grams butter, softened
2 large eggs
1½ cups high-grade flour
¼ teaspoon salt

Glaze and topping
2 tablespoons caster sugar
1 tablespoon boiling water
1 tablespoon pastry sugar grains (see The French Pantry opposite) or similar
few slices glacé fruits (choice is up to you)

Put the ingredients into the bowl of the bread machine in the order listed in your bread machine's manual. For mine the order was: yeast, sugar, water, butter, eggs, flour and salt. Set the bread machine to 'dough only' setting, and set it to work.

Turn the dough out onto a floured surface and gently deflate it. Roll into a 40cm length, dampen one end with a little water and join the ends together to form a circle. Transfer to a greased baking tray. If using a token (*fève*), push one into the dough from underneath. Cover with a clean tea towel and leave for 15 minutes to rise again.

Preheat the oven to 220°C and set the rack in the middle.

With scissors, make 8–10 small cuts in the top of the dough. Place the gâteau in the oven, turning it immediately down to 190°C. Bake in the preheated oven for 20–25 minutes or until golden, well risen and, if tapped from underneath, sounding hollow.

While baking, stir the caster sugar and boiling water together until the sugar dissolves; you may need to give it a few seconds in the microwave. Brush the glaze on top of the hot gâteau and sprinkle with the sugar grains or sliced glacé fruits. Cool on a wire rack.

This is best eaten on the day it is made.

Note to Cooks
Bread-making instructions will vary from brand to brand. Please refer to your instruction manual for any procedural variations.

janvier

France was beginning to work her charm
on us; our frantic rush-everywhere family
was adjusting to a slower pace of life.

As January dragged on, I found the lack of festive celebrations disheartening. I had anticipated that Christmas, New Year and Twelfth Night would be celebrated with zest and passion in rural France. If they were, it was behind closed doors; not one weathered shutter opened.

On New Year's Eve, we had a roaring fire to ward off the sub-zero temperatures, drank the delicious local Madiran wine and watched, for possibly the thirty-third time, a Harry Potter movie, before sleeping the New Year in!

The only folk we saw in the first weeks of the New Year were the bakers at the *boulangerie* – the French cannot live without their daily baguette – and the market stall-holders. This weekly ritual was often my only outing and I greeted the opportunity with excitement and relief.

As I wanted to get to know the stallholders, I created a page with pictures of our family – and the All Blacks logo for this passionate rugby area – telling them who we were and why we were there; that we spoke no French but that we were trying. I handed this out as I went along and managed to mumble my way through buying sufficient food to ensure we didn't go hungry! It was an inspired way to help break down the invisible barrier.

When kids are having fun, they rarely feel the cold. Although the temperature stayed mainly below 8°C during the days, they were happy to meet up with the village kids and ride their bikes all day; we hardly saw them unless they needed food. Caixon's mercifully mainly traffic-free checkerboard laneways were great for them to ride along and I loved being able to let a five-year-old scamper off with her brother and his friends.

Snow fell in the mountains just before school returned and out came the skiers, including us, the sand 'n' surf-loving Kiwis. As it was the children's first time on snow – picturesque mountain snow – we stuck to tobogganing. In Tarbes (our closest town), we survived a one-hour-long queue at ridiculously low temperatures so that Jean-Luc and Olive-Rose could try ice skating. Tarbes, like many European towns, creates temporary ice rinks when it freezes and everyone comes out to play . . . or fall over, as was the case with our two. They had a ball.

We visited Lourdes, about an hour away. Catholics are well versed in the story of Bernadette Soubirous, to whom the Virgin Mary is said to have appeared in 1858 and told her where to find a spring with miraculous healing powers. Now it is the site of the Grotte de Massabielle, which attracts many thousands of people who come each year to touch, pray, seek a miracle and 'take the waters'.

PAGE 44: A nearby country barn in need of repair.

THESE PAGES, CLOCKWISE FROM TOP LEFT: A villager en route to the local market; the village of Argelès-Gazost, which lies in the Azun Valley; first-time skiers at Hautacam; repaired communal village lavoir for washing clothes; chickens at the market, ready for sale; firemen making crêpes for a fundraiser at Vic-en-Bigorre market.

Lourdes contains two very different towns. The upper side is very modern and stylish but downhill, towards the river Gave de Pau, Lourdes has aged and looks slightly tired. Narrow, roughly paved streets are lined with tacky souvenir shops selling one-euro bottles of holy water, plastic religious trinkets and forlorn, dusty postcards. In summer, it seethes with visitors, so I was pleased we went in winter.

As an altar server at our church at Vic-en-Bigorre, Jean-Luc made some good friends who invited him to join their chess club and basketball team. I watched the three cherubic, robed boys chatter during Father Thierry-Joseph's long-winded sermon, oblivious to the solemnity of the occasion. Sometimes the deacon would scowl, but I was quietly delighted that Jean-Luc was smiling and making friends.

Despite the lack of school sports team events here, we were making headway with activities for our children. Chess lessons provided Jean-Luc with another avenue to learn French, but best of all he found his dad shared the same interest. France was beginning to work her charm on us; our frantic rush-everywhere city family was adjusting to a slower pace of life.

Olive-Rose, at only five, was happy at home but, like so many little girls, was horse mad. We enrolled her at a local riding club where the lessons were in French, giving Olive-Rose further opportunities to learn the language. For 10 euros (NZ$15.00) she had a weekly 1½-hour lesson with half a dozen other little girls. Olive-Rose's first lesson was getting a handle on the word *arrête* (stop) so that Tea Bag, her shaggy chestnut pony, didn't spend so much of the class with his nose in the rear of the horse in front!

Change comes when least expected. My son had always had long hair and it was only under sufferance that he would get even a fringe trim. However, when it came to returning to school, he asked to have it all cut off. I said it was up to him. His new look was more than just a haircut; it was a way to blend in better with the other boys. Being English-speaking was tough; having long hair had made him even more different. Back at school, there were unexpected slaps on the back from his friends. Jean-Luc was finding ways to clear his own hurdles to fit in better.

With school underway, teachers Marie-Paule and Camille, very aware of Jean-Luc's isolation, suggested a Kiwi afternoon tea for all 47 children. Beyond the All Blacks and kiwifruit, the local folk knew very little about New Zealand. Since French women rarely bake, the teachers thought my home-made cakes and biscuits would help break down some barriers.

With the children's help, I conjured up lamingtons, afghans, scones with jam and crème fraîche, classic Otago cheese rolls, sausage rolls and fairy bread. We also gave each child a New Zealand lapel pin, a huge hit. Everything was devoured; the Otago cheese rolls, prepared from onion soup mix which had come with us from home, and the other treats were new taste sensations for them but they loved it all! Cooking for this many in my minimally equipped kitchen and making do with different ingredients was a trial but it was worthwhile.

THIS PAGE: *Scenes from the holy town of Lourdes.*
FOLLOWING PAGE: *Preparing the Kiwi afternoon tea in my 'hobbit-sized' kitchen.*

Jean-Luc was, we hoped, on the way to making new friends, but Warwick's and my world was still pretty much friendless. The language barrier was enormous, and there were other factors too. Most immigrants in our area – and there were quite a few – were retirees, Francophiles from Britain seeking a quieter, slower life. They were all characters but most were without children, so their world was very different to ours.

Local parents work long hours, dropping kids at school at 7.30 a.m. and collecting them after work around 5.30 p.m. In winter, they stay in their cars, so there is no opportunity for school gate conversations; nor, in the absence of children's winter sport, is there a way to strike up sideline acquaintances.

Socialising is different too. There's no popping over for a coffee; you make an appointment to visit. Tea is served any time from 4 p.m. to 6 p.m. and is a cup of tea with cake; *apéros* (apéritifs) are from 5 p.m. to 7 p.m., as dinner will then be cooked for the family, to be served at 8 p.m. It is all very structured. There are no coffee shops or cafés where mothers and babies or girlfriends do mid-morning coffee. Bars are open, but their early morning customers are tradesmen having a coffee and bread stick before work; and they close in the afternoon.

However, in Maubourguet, a pretty village just 10 minutes from Caixon, I struck up a friendship with the Café du Central bar owner, Melanie, and her waitress, Coco. Overwhelmed by everything about the foreign environment and with Warwick again in New Zealand, I was sitting alone and miserable when the two girls came to my rescue with hugs, smiles and extra-large cups of *café grand crème*, making me feel so welcome. The bar became my refuge where, with the aid of my French–English dictionary and local newspapers, I could begin to learn some French. I spoke the language so badly that I created much mirth for the locals – how was I to know that 'preservative' in French translated to condom!

The other likely place to meet English speakers was the supermarket, which is how I met Brits Kate and Chris Coulson who, with their children Tana (named after Umaga) and India, had recently set up home in Lahitte-Toupière, a village in the hills behind us.

Our children were of similar age, got on well and all enjoyed being outside. Kate had established yoga classes, which I joined enthusiastically – as, surprisingly, did Warwick. I am not sure his body knew the word 'stretch' when he started! He'd never have dreamt of doing it in New Zealand. Classes were in French, which Kate speaks fluently, so I was often at odds with the other members of the class, causing many smiles. As well as our angels Graham and Irene, at last we had found some friends.

The Coulsons' property lies on one of the pilgrimage routes to Santiago de Compostela and Chris was converting their rambling farmhouse on seven hectares with barn and pool into a *gîte* (independent farmhouse stay) offering bed and breakfast. Kate was hoping to set up a yoga retreat. They are among a number of young couples who have moved to the area: their money goes further, the children become bilingual and can later undertake tertiary education in France or England, and they have left the madding crowd behind.

The month drew to a close with torrential rain and sub-zero Arctic blasts. The *fossés* (ditches) that flanked the laneways and the fields overflowed and Caixon was flooded in. Cold as it was, we all had fun cycling and watched our traveller neighbours canoe down Rue Longue! I wandered around my abandoned garden, which was drenched and frozen; it would be another month or more before I took out my *Yates Garden Guide*. This winter was proving to be very long.

The kids were getting tired of stews, especially the tough, chewy versions I was serving up. One night my son, always direct, asked what exactly it was I did for a job. When I said 'cook', he suggested I was not doing it very well! Desperate to understand the cuts of meat, I emailed home and help came via associates of Beef and Lamb New Zealand in Paris. By the end of the month the stews were becoming more palatable and we could move on from the safety of Bolognese on pasta!

To add variety I opted for duck, which was remarkably cheap – this was Gascony, the home of duck foie gras. Rabbit and Label Rouge chicken (see page 54) were both a tad expensive but, oh, the flavour . . . divine! Winter vegetables and fruit, crowding the stalls, were similar to what we would expect to find back in Kiwi supermarkets. The apple varieties were outstanding, especially the Chantecler which I would bake, with no added water, until they collapsed into a soft mound of golden slices which, when served with local *fromage blanc* (soft cheese with a yoghurt-like texture), were almost ambrosial. Bittersweet Seville oranges, briefly available, made just the best marmalade, which I used to glaze locally farmed pork belly. Other than that our diet was little different from what we would enjoy in a Kiwi winter. Dried beans were unappreciated and even when I snuck green lentils into the casseroles to encourage trial, they were painstakingly picked out by little people! Converting my family into duck confit and Tarbais bean-loving Gascon gourmets was going to take time!

Dark cold nights did not deter the circus from performing in Maubourguet and on another freezing night we found the market square filled by the classic striped big top, six enormous, spotless Kenworth trucks, each towing one or more trailers, and sundry caravans. On show were five majestic tigers, well-groomed dancing horses, Asian elephants and – best of all – a dromedary, on which the children were able to have a ride during the intermission. Trapeze artists, acrobats, clowns, jugglers and all the other traditional acts were awe-inspiring for two kids who normally only see animals at a zoo, and who had never watched trapeze artists in action. Complete with popcorn, this authentic travelling circus was fantastic!

As we found our car by torchlight, the children, cheeks flushed with the midnight chill, excitedly chattered about their favourite act and January finished on a happy note.

Of bunnies and chooks . . .

Jean-Luc wanted to try rabbit, so I bought one complete with head and beady eyes. At 18 euros it would not be a regular purchase! Madame had half-wrapped it when she enquired if I wanted the innards. I'm sure that she knew the answer before asking the question . . . and she was right! Rabbit heart, liver and kidneys were not in my planned recipe. I also splashed out on a 15-euro Label Rouge chicken, intact with head, feet and innards; this time I felt I should at least say 'yes' to the livers, lest I let my profession down!

Back home, Olive-Rose shrieked with delight when she saw Peter and Hennie with heads on, eyes intact and innards to examine. The following photo shoot got completely out of hand. However, it was fun teaching the kids about food that does not come skinned, boned, portion-controlled, plastic-wrapped and branded with ticks or with warnings; food as it should be sold, au naturel.

They helped prepare the stuffing for the rabbit – herbs, breadcrumbs, prunes and Armagnac. When I produced the darning needle to sew it up, to ensure the stuffing remained inside its belly, the children fell about in mirth . . . sewing up a rabbit!

We wrapped Peter in local, unsmoked cured bacon and baked him to perfection. Hennie was seasoned with sage, bay and thyme from my winter herb garden, slathered with delicious butter with big flakes of salt blended through it and roasted to a deep honey brown, sending a tantalising aroma wafting through the house. Simple food never tasted so good. The children were taken aback at the dark meat on the legs of the chicken and the more intense flavour – a real chicken, like the ones I recall from my youth.

Label Rouge chickens

As the result of a free-range production programme developed by the government in the mid-twentieth century, to be assigned 'Label Rouge' chickens must be produced according to criteria that include genetics (traditional breeds known to produce high-quality meat), natural cereal-based feed free of growth hormones, etc., duration of growth and conditions of farming. They are killed at around twice the age of factory birds (see also page 56).

Regarded as the ultimate French chook, Poulet de Bresse is produced to exacting standards at small farms in a limited area around Bresse in the Rhône-Alpes region. It was the first livestock to be granted AOC (see page 224) and thus protected under French and European law. The status was applied on the basis of the unique flavour of the birds achieved through growing conditions and locally produced grains.

Gascon black chicken

In nearby Puydarrieux, just beyond Trie-sur-Baïse on the border of the Hautes-Pyrénées and the Gers, Xavier Abate, a flamboyant ex-Parisian with charisma to burn, returned to the area of his youth. With the help of local farmers like Sophie Deffis, his mission is to stem the decline of the Noire d'Astarac Bigorre (Gascon black chicken), a breed that provides poultry of exceptional flavour. Like so many specialised breeds of animal, black chickens lost out in the 1950s to faster-growing commercial varieties, but now professionals and amateurs are joining forces to bring the breed back.

Sophie joined Xavier in 2003 and from only a handful has bred her flock up to a cluckingly noisy 350 fowls. The Noire d'Astarac Bigorre, with elegant black plumage that shines like a guardsman's boots, run free under hazelnut trees on this peaceful valley farm during the day and at night rest under cover, safe from predators. They are truly free range.

Chickens are culled at six months for a virgin cock and eight months for a capon (castrated male). The birds are processed by hand; only the body feathers are plucked and those of the tail and the head are left on. They are gutted before being aged in a cool room for three to four weeks. The resulting creamy, pinkish-hued flesh has a firm texture with an intense, almost gamey flavour. On the day I visited, chef Philippe Piton from the local starred restaurant Le Rive Droite poached both the breast (at 63°C for 25 minutes) and the eggs (at 65°C for 1 hour 25 minutes) in the oven. To my astonishment, the eggs were soft, almost jellied in consistency when cooked this way, and Philippe served them and the chicken with Pommes Parmentier (butter-tossed, fried cubed potatoes), a meal of sensational flavour.

Chefs and restaurateurs throughout France and other European markets purchase these birds, which carry Slow Food accreditation. They are wrapped like a Christmas cracker in a traditional pastel-dyed honeycombed tea towel, with stamp of origin and tail and head feathers on to guarantee provenance.

Jean-Luc and Olive-Rose learned more than they ever would at home. They had fun with Sophie on the farm, and gained from Xavier a respect for the production process before savouring the finished article in a meal that would have broken the credit card limit in Paris. On a farm in the rolling Gers, with laughter and locals, it was a priceless experience.

School Days

Jean-Luc's temporary misery highlighted the considerable differences in the schooling between France and New Zealand, both culturally and educationally. Schools run to a very set routine in France. Each village primary school is partnered with a *garderie* (daycare) and the running of both is a major function of the town hall and the Mayor. All three are usually in the same building or next door. The *garderie* provides before and after school care and serves the lunches. Because parents here work long, hard hours, usually in one of the larger towns or cities some distance away, the village school's *garderie* doors open from 7.30 a.m., when pupils may be dropped off, until pick-up time between 6 p.m. and 6.30 p.m. Here they are strictly cared for by *agents des écoles* (school supervisors) who are also responsible for the children's daily well-being, serving lunch and afternoon tea, setting up games and activities, and managing accounts (16 euros per term – NZ$24 – for our two). In many ways, the *garderie* moulds the children in the ways of the school and village.

Kids move to class at around 9 a.m., and at Jean-Luc's school this meant standing, rain, hail or shine, in single file outside the school door. Then, on the last stroke of nine o'clock by the village church clock, the teacher opens the door and welcomes each child individually. Olive-Rose's classroom was across the corridor from the *garderie*, but was not open for pupils until just before 9 a.m.

Pupils sit at individual tables, and the only time they speak is when they are spoken to. For Jean-Luc, accustomed to a noisy room, a table with friends and tasks to do as a group, this set-up was truly different and very lonely. Olive-Rose had small chairs at her school in New Zealand, so the big table and chair immediately made her feel all grown-up, ready to learn.

The 90-minute lunchtime was also new territory. Four courses are served to each child from the day they start school. The meal begins with *légumes* (vegetables), then meat or protein in some form, followed by cheese – often smelly, according to the kids – and finally dessert, which could be yoghurt, fruit or a slice of cake. My kids balked at many of the choices – cucumber or grated carrot drenched in vinaigrette, dried legumes or *haricots verts* (green beans) in a garlic sauce, Gascony's vegetable soup Garbure (see page 30), or liver or kidneys in sauce. They were certainly having their taste buds tested! Once finished, the children help with dishes, followed by a compulsory 15-minute digestion time before play, which was almost always inside. Used to netball courts, soccer fields, rugby balls and skipping ropes – even in winter – my two found being indoors most of the time constricting.

In the first few weeks, with the no-nonsense attitude to work, Jean-Luc was on the biggest learning curve of his short life; he could not do the mathematics at all. In France it's all about basics (I thought this refreshing): tables, addition, subtraction, multiplication and long division. All is done in an orderly fashion, much as it has been done for many years, showing all workings neatly on graph paper in pen. Jean-Luc's teacher was rather dismayed at his lack of maths knowledge for his age, but she had patience and kindness and gave him extra help.

Jean-Luc also needed help with his handwriting. French children learn cursive script from age four or five using graph-like paper, which helps them achieve a lovely rounded writing style. Coming from where a child needed to get a 'pen licence' to move from pencil to ballpoint, and only ever printed, this was another task Jean-Luc had to get the hang of – and quickly. At home, I revisited my youth and had the kids do copybook exercises to bring them up to speed. Why is such a basic neglected in New Zealand?

The teachers are strict and expect formal manners. They are addressed by the term *maîtresse* (teacher) and children are expected to stand when speaking to them. While Jean-Luc floundered with the rules, his father and I were quietly quite pleased about the formality of the school structure.

Tartiflette

This dish – served in chalets up and down the Hautes-Pyrénées – is certainly skiing fodder. Before refrigeration, when little fresh food was available in the colder months, standard commodities that would keep well in the cool room, such as onions, potatoes, *jambon* or bacon and cheese, were always there. A Tartiflette embodies so much of what we found in this area – simple, honest ingredients combined to make good food – and the final taste was always better than it looked. Don't get too carried away with unnecessary garnishes; indeed our food was rarely ever served garnished with pestos or salsas, drizzles or dustings, pinches or splashes.

Prep time: 15 minutes   Cooking time: 30 minutes   Serves: 4–5

200 grams thick-cut bacon rashers (smoked bacon is best; dry without too much fat)
1 large onion, peeled and finely sliced (if not large, use two)
1–1.25 kilograms waxy potatoes, cut into thick slices or chunks (peeling is optional)
500 grams Reblochon cheese (remove the rind for a less pungent final taste)

Cut the bacon crosswise into thick pieces and pan-fry in a dash of oil in a large ovenproof frying-pan. Set the bacon aside, leaving the fat from the bacon in the pan.

Add the onion and cook over a moderate heat, stirring until softened and browned a little – not too much or the onion will burn and leave a bitter taste.

Increase the heat, add the potato and stir it in the fat until it begins to sizzle and brown a little. Lower the heat, cover and cook until the potato is tender, stirring occasionally so it browns evenly. Scatter the bacon over.

Slice the cheese thinly and arrange on top of the potato. At this stage you can either leave the pan on the stovetop over a low heat for about 10 minutes and allow the cheese to gradually melt its way down through the potatoes, or place the frying-pan into a preheated, moderately hot oven for about the same time until the cheese melts.

If you want more sauce, spoon some crème fraîche generously over the potatoes before arranging the cheese on top. For a lighter version use stock instead of crème fraîche.

Serve as is with a gutsy wine.

The French Pantry

Reblochon, a washed-rind cheese, melts to a nutty creaminess and is the authentic cheese for a Tartiflette; some brands sell it as *Fromage du Tartiflette*. Its home is the Haute-Savoie, on the eastern border with Switzerland and Italy, and it is comparatively docile in flavour when compared with other washed-rind cheeses such as Munster.

Armagnac-glazed Baked Rabbit

Rabbits run wild behind Au Palouque, and in an area reliant on crop production, their presence is not entirely welcome, so they are a favourite for the family oven. Their lean, well-flavoured meat goes well with herbs of any season – although in winter my garden was limited to sage, thyme and parsley – dried fruits, of which my preference is for prunes or apricots, and members of the onion family, leek or onions and garlic. The bacon must be streaky: the fat carries flavour and adds moisture to the rabbit. Armagnac – the fiery spirit produced in that area – ensures a shiny glaze and beguiles the palate, and is especially suited to those who may find rabbit a little unnerving. In place of Armagnac try Cognac, although it is expensive; or use brandy mixed with equal quantities of vodka, the former for flavour and the latter for glazing.

Prep time: 30 minutes   Cooking time: 1¼ hours   Serves: 4

1 large rabbit (to feed four)
100 grams butter
1 medium onion, peeled and finely diced (or use a trimmed leek for a milder taste)
2 cloves garlic, crushed, peeled and mashed to a paste with a pinch of salt
1–1½ cups fresh breadcrumbs (I prefer good-quality white bread)
2 teaspoons chopped fresh sage (1 teaspoon if using dried sage)
a handful of chopped fresh parsley
1 loosely packed cup moist prunes, stoned and roughly chopped
¾ cup Armagnac (or spirits of your choice)
8 long rashers streaky bacon, rind removed

Prune gravy
2 tablespoons flour
2 cups chicken stock

Preheat the oven to 190°C. Set the rack in the middle of the oven.

Remove any internal bits left in from the sale of the rabbit – probably none, but you never know.

Melt 1–2 tablespoons of the butter in a frying-pan and gently cook the onion and garlic over a low heat until very soft, without allowing it to brown. Stir in the breadcrumbs, herbs and a quarter of the prunes, and season well with salt and pepper. Place the remaining prunes into the Armagnac (or other spirits), and set aside; you will need this to make the gravy later on.

Stuff the rabbit with the breadcrumb mixture and secure the stuffing by closing the two sides using toothpicks or, as I much prefer, sewing the rabbit up with a coarse thread and

a darning needle: this way there's no chance of any stuffing spilling out.

Wrap the bacon around the rabbit and tie everything up with a few rounds of string – make sure it is not plastic string – to keep the rabbit neat and tidy. Place the bunny on its side in a roasting dish and spread with the remaining butter.

Bake in the middle of the preheated oven for about 1 hour – the time will depend on the size of the rabbit. Turn the rabbit once during cooking time to ensure it cooks evenly. To check for doneness, use a sharp, thin-bladed knife and make a cut at the leg joint; it should be moist and juicy but not pink and under-done.

Pour off the fat from the roasting dish and keep to one side. Carefully pour 2–3 tablespoons (no more, it's fierce stuff) of the Armagnac (that the prunes are soaking in) over the rabbit and flambé. Once the flames are exhausted, place the rabbit on a plate and keep warm while making the gravy.

Return 3 tablespoons of reserved fat to the roasting dish. Any remaining fat can be kept and used to roast potatoes or other root vegetables at another time. Place the roasting dish over a direct heat, stir in the flour and cook for about a minute until frothy. Gradually add the chicken stock, prunes and remaining Armagnac and simmer, stirring constantly, to make a smooth gravy. Season with salt and pepper. If you would like a thinner gravy, add more stock.

Remove the string and with a cook's knife cut the rabbit into six portions. Cut across the rabbit at the back legs and under the front legs, leaving the middle loin section which, if large, can be cut in half crosswise. Then cut each portion in half. Serve a mix of the pieces with decent spoonfuls of the stuffing and coat generously with the gravy. Mashed potatoes, well-baked pumpkin and seasonal greens make excellent accompaniments to the rabbit.

Country Fig Bread

The French love their bread. Village *boulangeries* are often open seven days a week, although only mornings on a Sunday. Pascal, our *boulanger* at Maubourguet, opens on Christmas Day and Good Friday morning to cope with the requirements of these festive days; bakers here work long and hard. On a Wednesday, we indulged in fig bread from Marciac, a charming *bastide* (fortified) village not far from Caixon, where the Wednesday market, held within the town walls as it has been for centuries, featured more than the usual number of colourful craftspeople selling gaily patterned hand-made bags, clothes, artwork and knitted goods, as well as tables of second-hand children's books. It was our market for buying gifts and any mid-week supplies, although Jean-Luc would routinely be found emptying his pocket money on Asterix books; we now have so many, I think I can set up shop myself!

Prep and cooking time: about 3 hours   Makes: 1 loaf

1½ cups tepid water
1 tablespoon sugar (brown or white)
1 good teaspoon salt (this is essential)
500 grams flour (use 450 grams white high-grade flour and 50 grams rye flour)
1 generous tablespoon active yeast mixture (also called bread yeast mix)
8–10 moist dried figs, roughly chopped (do not use glacé figs)

Put the water, sugar, salt, flour and yeast into the bowl of the bread machine and set the machine to regular standard bake. (See Note to Cooks on page 41.) Allow the machine to do the work for you. Check, once the machine gets going, that there is the right amount of liquid or flour. I'm constantly opening the lid of my bread machine – at the beginning – to make sure the dough texture is right, and I add more liquid or flour as needed. However, once the dough begins to prove for baking, avoid opening the lid as the shock of cold air will chill the dough and it will collapse somewhat.

The machine will beep towards the end of the initial kneading phase, at which time add the figs. You could also add them at the beginning, so long as you do not mind the dried fruit being well mashed. I quite like it this way, especially if I am going to use the bread for toasting, as large chunks of figs tend to burn in the toaster.

If you plan to make the fig bread by hand, it is best to dissolve the yeast in the warm water first; I always find it hard to get the yeast granules to dissolve completely without this step. Stir the yeast into the water and set aside until the mixture turns slightly porridge-like and has formed frothy bubbles on top.

Sift the flour, salt and sugar onto a bench top – make sure you have a large clean space to work on. Spread the flour out, making a very large circle in the centre. Into this, pour all the frothy yeast water. Make sure there are no gaps in the flour walls lest you have an unexpected flood. Using the fingertips of one hand only, keeping the free hand clean, stir the flour into the well. Once all the flour is incorporated, bring the dough together, add the figs and knead well until the dough is soft and spongy.

Rest, covered, for 45–60 minutes or until the dough is well risen. Turn out, deflate gently, shape and place on a greased baking tray or alternatively place in a well-greased, large (12cm x 26cm) loaf tin. Some fig slices arranged on top add a nice finish. Leave in a warm place for about 45 minutes to rise until doubled in bulk.

Preheat oven to 200°C.

Bake fig bread in the preheated oven for 25–35 minutes, depending on size and shape. To tell when the bread is cooked, tap it underneath; it should make a hollow sound.

Once cooked, cool on a wire rack. It's delicious served warm with *jambon* (salt-cured and air-dried ham) and soft cheese.

The French Pantry

French *pain de campagne* (country bread) contains rye flour. The amount varies from bakery to bakery and also among the brands selling bread mixes for home use, somewhere from 5 per cent up to 30 per cent; it adds a distinctive warm flavour and gives a honey hue to the finished bread. While you cannot clearly taste the rye, the bread is truly more-ish, especially when toasted. Prepared bread mixes and bread flours abound on supermarket shelves and in markets in France, making bread-making at home easy. Bread machines were common in the area we lived in, no doubt because of the closure of so many small village bakeries and the growth of the expat community.

Caixon Daube

A Daube takes its name from the ceramic-lidded dish in which it is cooked. This is a hearty winter stew prepared from wine-drenched beef or lamb and flavoured with onions, carrots, olives, tomatoes and sweet spices of cinnamon, cloves and peppercorns, along with the perfumed rind and sweet juice of an orange. In our area, the local red wine, Madiran AOP, is so gutsy that it is often blended with Merlot to soften out the tannins, but it's ideal for this stew, which needs long, slow cooking and plenty of spuds to sponge up all the delicious sauce.

Prep time: 30 minutes   Marinating time: overnight   Cooking time: 3½–4 hours Serves: 8

1.25 kilograms beef for casseroling (crosscut blade, chuck or gravy beef are good)
3–4 large onions, peeled and sliced (use brown for best flavour)
4 good-size carrots, peeled and thickly sliced
6 large cloves garlic, crushed, peeled and sliced
150 grams thick-cut smoked bacon, diced (*jambon* makes a great substitute)
½ cup each good-quality green and black olives (pit them only if you want to)
4 large tomatoes, halved, deseeded and sliced, or 1 x 400 gram can chopped tomatoes
pared rind and juice of 1 large orange
1 teaspoon peppercorns (use whichever colour you have)
½ teaspoon whole cloves
⅓ stick cinnamon (if using ground cinnamon use a scant ¼ teaspoon)
1 bouquet garni (see page 31)
750 ml bottle gutsy red wine
about 1 cup beef stock (you may need a little more)

Cut the beef into large pieces and layer it in a deep casserole with the onion, carrot, garlic, bacon or *jambon*, olives and tomato, placing the orange rind and juice, peppercorns, cloves, cinnamon and bouquet garni in the middle layers. I am happy to have whole spices in my Daube, but you can also tie them in a muslin bag, place somewhere in the layers and remove before serving.

Pour the wine and beef stock over: the ingredients should be just covered in the liquid. Cover and refrigerate at least overnight.

Preheat the oven to 200°C and place the rack below the centre.

Before cooking the Daube, check the liquid level and add more beef stock if required – the liquid should just cover the ingredients.

Place the Daube – tightly covered to keep all the flavour in – in the preheated oven and cook for 30 minutes. Turn the oven down to 140°C and allow the casserole to simmer slowly for 3–3½ hours or until the meat falls to pieces.

Remove from the oven and carefully drain the cooking liquid into a saucepan. Keep the Daube warm while you boil the liquid down until reduced by half to one-third, or until thick and syrupy. Pour over the Daube and serve.

Classically a Daube is served with a gremolata. This is a mix of chopped fresh parsley, lemon rind and fresh garlic, and it adds a delightful freshness to the slow-cooked dish. I always used whatever was to hand; orange rind, chopped black olives and parsley are also a nice combination.

The French Pantry
This is an ideal dish to cook in a crock-pot or slow cooker. Allow 7–8 hours on low or 5–6 hours on high. You will need to pour off the cooking liquid and reduce as above.

février

Locals take winter in their stride,
but for us, new to the concept,
hibernating was a struggle.

I FELT THE ISOLATION MORE KEENLY IN FEBRUARY than in any other winter month. I had expected life would be more cheerful once the January cold had passed but, while New Zealand was basking under cloudless blue skies and all-day sunshine, Europe was experiencing one of its worst winters on record. Ferocious winds, chilling rains and unprecedented dumpings of snow resulted in us often being snowed or flooded in.

The mountains to which we looked in admiration each day were rarely visible. Snow clouds hung low and, with avalanche warnings out for most of the region's local ski fields, *gendarmes* (military policemen) patrolled the roads to ensure no wayward travellers got through.

Snow, thick, white, fluffy and very cold, came to Caixon overnight; we did not hear it fall, but I certainly heard the cries of delight when the children opened the shutters to let in what little light there was. As we couldn't get out of the village, there would be no school so it was time for making a snowman. Sadly, as quickly as the snow came, it was gone the next morning leaving the ground sodden and pathways covered in mud-coloured slush. Even though it lasted only one day, the snow was a real novelty for us all and it created laughter and fun memories at a time when cabin fever was taking its toll.

Locals take winter in their stride, but for us, new to the concept, hibernating was a struggle. Pizza and charades at the Coulsons' home boosted our flagging spirits. We caught up with world news, chatted generally and compared notes on schooling and other aspects of life here. While we could read all about home online, we truly missed the radio with familiar voices and local issues; funny, really, what we missed from our Auckland lives. We had thought we would be more independent. Skype was a blessing for communicating with family and friends and reducing the distance between us.

Larreule school's *loto* night was the one event in February when the entire village, locals and itinerants, came together; think bingo, but in French. It began at 9 p.m., when most New Zealand kids are tucked up asleep, and we joined in, providing a large box of cosmetics from Warwick's company as part of the main prize.

The village hall was bursting at the seams. I have no idea whence they all came. Some we recognised as parents supporting the school, but more than half were travellers, who apparently use these events as a way to get free goods – and they were seriously competitive. Prizes were outstanding by our standards. Olive-Rose's one-line

PAGE 72: *Winter snow blankets the front lawn at Au Palouque.*

THESE PAGES, CLOCKWISE FROM TOP LEFT: *The romantic-looking village of Saint-Émilion, Bordeaux; the kids build a snowman in our front yard; snow-kissed fields at Larreule; where there's a Frenchman at a market, there's bound to be a dog; boats at the Hondarribia, Spain; mini chorizo-style sausages wrapped in thin slices of aubergine.*

FOLLOWING PAGE, CLOCKWISE FROM TOP LEFT: *Dried corn kernels make excellent tokens; lolly kebabs for the children – simplicity is key at community gatherings; our family joins the loto night at Larreule.*

win was a package that included trendy jeans, book vouchers, movie tickets, a three-way puzzle, a bead set, balloons and crackers. There were more than 50 such prize packages; local businesses had been really supportive. With over 1500 euros raised, it was a huge success for a school with a roll of 47 children. I must mention the refreshments: mostly alcohol-free drinks and crêpes for adults, and lolly kebabs and water for the young.

Since there was no school in France on Wednesdays while we lived there, we were free for family adventures. On one such day we visited the delightful 'Cittaslow' *bastide* town of Mirande to show the children the unique design of mediaeval fortified towns. *Bastide* towns were mostly built in Gascony, as part of settling the remote wilderness of southwest France in the thirteenth and fourteenth centuries and to try to create trade. Usually rectangular, occasionally circular, they had common features in an arcaded square, a church, and a grid of streets running along the façades of the houses with alleyways going off at right-angles. Many have not survived, either through lack of population or destroyed in wartime.

Mirande is one of more than 100 towns worldwide that have chosen to follow a 'slow' life. The Slow Food movement awards the 'Cittaslow' label to towns that meet a stringent set of criteria. The label promotes a philosophy of a slower way of life, where appreciation of identity and local culture are the main objectives. At the fifteenth-century church of St Mary, we admired a similarly aged stained-glass window that filtered the winter sun onto us below. Grasping the age of such places is hard for many of us from down under, especially the kids – Jean-Luc struggles with the concept of our French home being older than European settlement in New Zealand!

Vic-Fezensac holds the first *feria* (Spanish for a series of bullfights) of this area around Pentecost, kick-starting the annual bullfighting season. The *feria* takes over the town, with a *course landaise* (see page 220) and bullfights over the whole weekend. Almost deserted on the day of our visit, during the festival the town is over-run with street parties, *bodegas* (outside bars) and restaurants that spill out onto the pavement. Somehow, it was hard to imagine such festivities in the constant foul weather.

On our way home, we took the route of the old Roman road through the valley of the Baïse to see the unique *tourasses* (towers) of the Gers. The reason for constructing these neat masonry towers has never been fully established. Suggestions include a trophy to celebrate a military victory or more likely for some religious purpose. The best one sits at the top of a hill in rolling countryside in the quaint village of Biran, which could truly have been the setting for *Chocolat*, the film of Joanne Harris's book. We played hopscotch on a cobblestoned street that led from the tower to an amazing church, while Warwick was off seeking help and learning the lesson of not filling the car up with petrol before a Sunday drive!

There are many *bastide* towns nearby, and we never tired of visiting them. Their history is remarkable and there is hope for their future. After both world wars, many people left farm and village life to seek jobs in the cities, deserting the wood-and-daub and stone houses. Now, some of them are retiring and returning to their roots. In addition, living a slower paced life in the southwest appeals to many self-employed Europeans, who can retire here without losing benefits under EU law. There are also families with children, where one partner commutes overseas to work in such industries as oil or construction.

School holidays were rocking around again – they come every six weeks here – and with Jean-Luc still somewhat miserable, I took him out a week early so that he could join me as camera assistant on a five-day, hands-on, dig-it-yourself Truffle Walk. Our hosts were charming Brits James and Diana Tamlyn, who have lived in a quaint French farmhouse cottage in the Lot region at the northern end of the Midi-Pyrénées for more than 17 years.

Our tour began with two days of walking through fallow pastures and wintering vineyards, over oak-clad *crêtes*, through picturesque villages and past grand châteaux. We dined on five- and seven-course truffle dinners and brunches with four other truffle enthusiasts. We hunted the elusive truffle with Jerome and his Australian border collie Farouq, and followed the journey of the culinary black gold through to the best-known truffle market at Lalbenque.

Here beret-clad French farmers line up to display their valuable cache in tiny red and white cloth-lined wicker baskets; 1200 euros per kilogram is the asking price. Once the cordon drops and buyers move in, the mêlée caused by more buyers than truffles is over in a flash. It was a truly exciting experience.

Cooking at the cottage where we were staying, Jean-Luc pondered whether doing long division by hand might not have been preferable to deveining an over-sized duck liver and eating snails in crème frâiche and a warm *gésier* (duck gizzard) and bacon salad. Some lessons, I told him, cannot be taught in the classroom. I am not sure he was totally convinced!

We all enjoyed the remainder of the school holidays, travelling around the area, taking in Bordeaux, skiing at Lourdes and biking in San Sebastián, despite the mercury seldom rising above two degrees.

In Bordeaux, we sampled and enjoyed delightful lesser-known wines of the wider region. Vincent, our guide to the region, and owner of Château Rousselle, was a seriously cool dude! Opposed to the aged and over-the-top AOC wine regulations, Vincent dismissed the Médoc with disdain, as . . . 'pfft', said almost with a spit. 'Novices, newcomers, their wine is made from a trendy new cross-bred grape, the Cabernet Sauvignon. In short,' he said, 'their wine is s—t!'

On the other hand, he described the wines of the Bourg and Blaye, where his own rustic family château looks out over the mud-coloured Gironde estuary, as 'true classics', 'pedigree' wines. What wonderful television this ruggedly handsome man would have made, with his long, wavy grey hair, a high-flying Parisian company director turned impoverished winemaker. Every spare corner of our car was loaded up with Vincent's truly delicious wine for the return trip.

Going home via San Sebastián was a soul-rejuvenating break. Jean-Luc's and Olive-Rose's taste buds were well challenged as we bar-hopped our way around a diverse selection of outlets serving *pintxo* (Basque-style tapas): fresh, crispy-coated deep-fried anchovies on skewers, prawn and crab tarts, tortillas (thick potato omelettes), slice after slice of *jamón* (ham), goat kebabs, sheep cheese tarts, smoked and marinated d'Espelette (a variety of chilli pepper, see page 280) and more.

February was nearly over and 1 March, which would mark the beginning of spring and school resuming, was only a few days away. Feeling optimistic after our joyful dose of Spanish sun, I hoped that by then I would be able to garden, that the food in the markets would move on from pumpkin, parsnips and potatoes and that I would see more locals out and about. February with such harsh weather had been tough for everyone.

Les Truffes

The truffle, like no other food except maybe tripe, divides the world with a mere sniff! I confess that I am not a truffle aficionado and am unable to understand all the fuss. Nevertheless, for many the truffle is a culinary icon, rating with kopi luwak, foie gras, bird's nest soup or beluga caviar, each similarly loved or loathed; there doesn't seem to be any neutral ground!

Simply put, the truffle is the fruiting body of a fungus. It is host-specific and grows underground from May to July, when it will reach full size although not maturity, which takes a further five months. It is harvested in the latter months of winter. Once pigs were used to sniff out the truffle, but nowadays trained dogs, more nimble and easier to control, do the job.

For the serious truffle hunter with patience to spare, the truffle fly (*Suillia pallida*) can be an indicator of location. These slender, fluorescent-winged flies hover close to the ground, attracted by the truffles' scent. The males will be looking for a mate (in the way of males!) and, if luck has been on their side, the females are laying their eggs; the truffles provide food for the larvae.

Free-ranging animals were the original vehicle for spreading spores, but these days truffle growing is highly scientific. There are still small numbers of local foragers, who look for the 'burnt' patch under the tree as an indicator of truffle location. However, most growers in this area, which was once called Périgord, run mixed farms on which they plant an area of oak trees inoculated with Périgord black truffle (*Tuber melanosporum*) as a side venture with other income streams.

Once dug up, truffles survive for only a few days but it is possible to keep them under a layer of duck fat after using a toothbrush to brush off the dirt. Long keeping is not easy, although some opinion favours freezing them in a lidded jar of risotto rice and both can then be used.

For true opulence, slice fresh truffles wafer thin, sandwich two slices with soft, unsalted butter and serve sprinkled with flaky salt. A less extravagant approach is to grate fresh truffle over freshly cooked and buttered pasta, where a little goes a long way. If you are hesitant and need only a faint truffle flavour, place the truffle in a carton of eggs where it can buddy-up for the night and permeate the eggs' porous shell; serve the eggs scrambled or coddled. Simple is best, as with so many exotic foods. While truffle oil is a far cry from the real thing, for many it is the only affordable way to sample the flavour. Buy one of good quality and use quickly after opening; best drizzled over foods before serving.

Le Canard

In southwest France, on the tables of Gascony, *le canard* (duck) takes pride of place over any other meat. Scarcely a restaurant does not feature duck on the menu, and each week the biggest queues at our market were at the duck sellers. The traditional home of foie gras production is the Gers, the department next to us, where 4.5 million ducks and 120,000 geese are farmed annually for the *foie* (liver). In 2000, the European Union officially recognised the link between duck foie gras and the southwest by providing a protected geographical indication. This quality mark is in addition to the Label Rouge awarded to the southwest in 1989 and held by more than 900 Midi-Pyrénées producers.

Because of the French passion for foie gras – they produce about 19,000 tonnes a year from around 38 million ducks – there is an abundance of cuts of duck meat for the table. I do not wish to become involved in discussion of the ethics of the production of foie gras. However, as a cook, when foie gras was presented in a creative way, with a seasonal fruit accompaniment and a glass of the local Pacherenc du Vic-Bilh – sweet wine – it was unreservedly delicious, like nothing I had ever tasted (and the price of which meant I rarely did!). Here's a summary of terms relating to foie gras and duck cuts with the best cooking styles.

Foie gras fundamentals

Foie gras is the liver of a goose or duck specifically fattened by force-feeding. Under the French Rural Code (2006), foie gras is recognised as part of the protected cultural and gastronomic heritage of France. While connoisseurs maintain that goose foie gras has a finer flavour, duck foie gras, which is easier to produce, is readily available and more affordable.

- *Entier* – whole foie gras available cooked or uncooked.
- *Bloc* – smaller pieces whipped and condensed to make a block, often containing truffles.
- *Mousse* – pieces puréed to make a smooth mousse.
- *Pâté* – mixed with meats such as pork and duck to make a pâté.
- *Mi-cuit* – also called semi-cooked, pasteurised foie gras, it is cooked and preserved to match its original texture and flavour as closely as possible.
- *Cuit* – whole foie gras cooked in its own fat in a sterilised jar or can. Stored for some time, like wine, it mellows.

Duck details

Rarely did I see roasted whole duck being served in a restaurant; with the number of ducks available, I suspect roasting the bird whole was more a home-cooking option. It was far more common to buy duck portions, which are easier to serve and each of which can be cooked appropriately.

- *Magret* – single duck breast: perfect for pan-frying, barbecued or salted and dried for antipasto. When the double breast is cut crosswise into thick slices, the result is the very popular *steak du magret*.
- *Aiguillettes* – the strip of fillet that lies under the main breast or *magret*. In chicken this is called the *suprème*. Perfect for quick cooking.
- *Cuisse de canard* – duck leg and thigh portions: roast or casserole.
- *Manchons* – duck wings: roast or casserole.
- *Coeur de canard* – duck hearts: grill or casserole.
- *Gésiers* – gizzards: grill or casserole.
- *Gras du canard* – duck fat: use for cooking confit, great for roasting potatoes.
- *Grattons de canard* – duck scratchings: as a garnish, best served warm.

Duck confit can be prepared from any of the above cuts: it refers to duck cooked in its own fat. It is then stored under a thick layer of the fat, canned, bottled or refrigerated.

Foie Gras Tarts with Apple and Fig

We fell upon Chez Gorka, a charming restaurant in the mediaeval village of Tillac, not far from us, after we had rummaged through the annual *vide-grenier* (flea market) in the cobblestoned, arcaded street of half-timbered houses. Unexpectedly, considering the restaurant's isolation, the menu selection was extensive, with *plat du jour* (dish of the day) choices celebrating the best of Basque, Spanish, Gascony and Bayonne cuisine. I seldom went past this tart, which over the eight months the restaurant was open – most close over winter here – came variously presented, although the same elements were always combined. It reflected a modern twist on the traditional foie gras and fig partnership and, like Gérard Bor's Tarbais Bean and Foie Gras Velouté (see page 286), I will miss Chez Gorka's lovely food and the village of Tillac. Uncooked foie gras could be bought frozen in slices, which were quick and easy to pan-fry, although canned foie gras will suffice for those of you who venture to try this fabulous recipe.

Prep time: 30 minutes   Cooking time: 40 minutes   Serves: 4

250 grams shortcrust pastry
1 white onion, peeled and diced (brown is too strong in flavour)
2 large Golden Delicious apples, peeled, cored and nicely diced
50 grams butter
¼ cup Armagnac or brandy
200 grams foie gras (canned is fine)
½ cup fig jam (plum jam is a good substitute)

Preheat the oven to 190°C. Grease 4 x 10 cm round tart tins.

Roll the pastry out on a lightly floured bench and use to line the base and sides of the tart tins. Trim away excess pastry. Line each pastry case with baking paper and fill with baking-blind material. Bake in the preheated oven for 10–12 minutes or until the edges of the pastry begin to brown. Remove the baking-blind material and return the tins to the oven to cook for a further 5–7 minutes or until the pastry is well cooked. Remove from the oven and leave to cool. When cold, the pastry cases can be kept in an airtight container for up to a week.

In a frying-pan, slowly cook the onion and apple in the butter so that they soften well, then caramelise. The onion must be well cooked. Add 3 tablespoons of the Armagnac and when the sizzling stops, remove from the heat.

When ready to serve, divide the onion mixture evenly among the tart cases and place on a tray in a 160°C oven to warm through.

Cut the foie gras into slices, and pan-fry in a non-stick frying-pan until well browned. Add the jam and remaining Armagnac, turning the pieces of foie gras to glaze. Divide the pieces evenly among the hot tarts, placing them on top and spooning a little glaze on each to serve.

Pork with Lentils, Ginger and Pears

The love of *jambon* – salt-cured and air-dried leg of ham on the bone – has ensured this area has a plentiful and economical supply of other pork cuts. *Épaule* (shoulder), *collet* (collar), *côtelettes* (cutlets and chops), *filet*, *poitrine* (chest), *jambonneau* (pork knuckle), *pied* (foot) and *tête* (head), along with sundry cuts like ears, snout and liver, were all readily available at the market and supermarket.

Prep time: 15 minutes   Cooking time: 2 hours   Serves: 8–10

1.5–1.75 kilograms pork roast, shoulder, loin or leg (skin removed)
6–7 cups vegetable or chicken stock (stock cubes and water is fine)
1 large or 2 small onions, peeled and finely chopped
2 large cloves garlic, crushed, peeled and finely chopped
6–8 cm piece fresh ginger, peeled and finely chopped, better still grated
5–6 ripe pears (any variety is fine)
1½ cups green lentils
1–2 cups jus or gravy (use packet-made for ease)

Preheat the oven to 190–200°C.

Place the pork and 2 cups of vegetable or chicken stock into a large, deep roasting dish. Season well with salt and pepper and cover with foil. Bake in the preheated oven for 1 hour.

Pan-fry the onion, garlic and ginger in a good knob of butter until the onion has softened. Halve the pears and peel if wished; I like the way the cooked flesh sits in the skin, which can act like a safety boat in case of overcooking. Leave the pears under water to which the juice of half a lemon has been added, until the meat is ready.

When the hour is up, remove the pork from the oven and pour in 4 cups of stock. Scatter the onion mixture and lentils around and nestle the pears into the lentils.

Return to the oven, this time without a cover, and cook for a further 1 hour or until the meat is cooked. The lentils should be cooked and there should be some liquid remaining with them. If the pork requires more cooking time, assess whether you need more stock to prevent the lentils from drying out.

Once the meat is cooked, transfer with the pears to a warmed serving dish. Stir the hot jus or gravy into the lentils to make a thick, chunky sauce. Serve the pork thickly sliced with a generous serving of lentils and a pear half.

Cauliflower and Truffle Velouté

The humble *chou-fleur* (cauliflower) seems in recent years to have slipped out of the limelight. The origin of this highly nutritious vegetable is obscure, although the old French name for it, *chou de Chypre* (Cyprus) may offer a clue. Luckily for us, the cauliflowers in the marketplaces here were of marvellous quality – tight flower buds, well wrapped in their green leaves – and were available pretty much all year round. We enjoyed them most often as a *potage*, although interestingly enough, when served as a vegetable, the broken pieces, only steamed and seasoned, reminded me of a cauliflower crumble rather than florets. Nonetheless, this member of the cabbage family has a gutsy flavour that marries well with truffle.

Prep time: 15 minutes   Cooking time: 30 minutes   Serves: 8

1 small onion, peeled and chopped; or 1 leek, white part only, chopped
50 grams butter
2 tablespoons flour
5–6 cups chicken stock
1 starchy potato, peeled and diced (avoid waxy potatoes)
500 grams cauliflower, cut into florets
2 egg yolks
½ cup cream
1 teaspoon finely chopped fresh truffle, or truffle oil

Gently cook the onion or leek in the butter in a large saucepan until very soft but not browned. Stir in the flour and cook for 1 minute in the butter and onion. Remove from the heat and gradually stir in 5 cups of stock; done this way you will avoid making starchy lumps in any thickened sauce. Add the potato and return to the heat to simmer for about 15 minutes until the potato is soft. At this point, add in the cauliflower and continue to simmer for around 10–12 minutes or only until the cauliflower is soft, no longer or your soup will turn a sallow shade of pink and gain a sulphurous taste. The time will depend on the freshness of the cauliflower and the size of the florets; be watchful.

Purée well. Return to the saucepan and add the remaining stock if you want a thinner soup.

Beat the egg yolks and cream together, quickly whisk into the soup, and reheat without boiling, lest the egg yolks scramble. Add the truffle just before serving and season with salt and white pepper – black is out of the question for this velvet cream-coloured soup.

Serve with crunchy croutons and a few cooked florets of cauliflower. For those who treasure indulgence, add an extra sliver of truffle before serving. I love the soup without truffle but garnished with crispy fried *jambon* or bacon.

Duck Confit with Raisin Jus

We ate duck confit as we might eat sausages at home – weekly. To my mind, this is one of the most enjoyable ways to prepare, cook and eat duck leg and thigh portions, especially in winter, and it's also an ideal dish to have with friends as it can be prepared well in advance and just baked on the night.

Prep time: 15 minutes   Brining time: 2 days   Cooking time: 2 hours   Serves: 4

4 duck leg and thigh portions
6 tablespoons coarse or flaky salt
2 bay leaves, crushed
1 teaspoon coarsely cracked peppercorns (any colour or a mix)
1 stick cinnamon, crushed
a few whole cloves
a few sprigs thyme
500–650 grams duck fat

Pat the duck portions dry with a paper towel and place in a dish or sealable plastic bag. Sprinkle over the salt, bay leaves, peppercorns, cinnamon, cloves and thyme and turn to coat the duck pieces well with the mixture. Refrigerate for two days, turning occasionally.

Remove the duck from the brine and wash well to remove any traces of salt. Pat dry with paper towel. Discard the salt.

Preheat the oven to 130°C.

Heat the duck fat in a flameproof casserole and, once melted, add the duck portions, making sure they sit well beneath the duck fat. Bring to a simmer.

Transfer the dish to the preheated oven and cook for 1¾–2 hours or until the meat shrinks well away from the bone. Carefully remove the duck from the duck fat and set aside. Strain the duck fat into a jug to allow any meat juices to settle below the fat. Keep the juice – it is wonderful for flavouring gravies, soups or casseroles.

Into the casserole or a dish that will snugly hold the duck portions, pour just enough duck fat to cover the base. Sit the duck portions on top and then cover with the remaining fat – the duck portions must be well covered. Refrigerate until required.

To serve, preheat the oven to 200°C and place the oven rack just above the centre. Lift the duck from the fat. Scrape off any fat clinging to the duck portions and, using a paper towel, wipe away as much as you can. Transfer the pieces to an oven tray.

Roast in the preheated oven for 25 minutes or until the duck is hot and the skin is crispy and golden. Serve with Poor Man's Sarladaise Potatoes and Raisin Jus (see page 92).

Poor Man's Sarladaise Potatoes

100 grams duck fat
1 kilogram waxy potatoes, peeled and cut into ½ cm-thick slices
2–3 rashers thick-cut bacon, diced (smoked has a better flavour) (optional)

In a wide frying-pan, heat the duck fat, and when hot add the potatoes. Cook until they brown in the duck fat, then lower the temperature and keep turning them regularly.

If wished, when the potatoes are half cooked, add diced bacon. Once tender, the potatoes will be a mix of whole slices and broken pieces, some well browned, others not. Season with parsley and, if you are game, stir through minced fresh garlic before serving.

Raisin Jus

1 cup good-quality chicken stock
1 cup red wine (we used the local Madiran AOC)
1 cup chicken gravy (packet-made is fine)
½ cup moist dried raisins

In a saucepan, simmer everything together until the mixture has reduced by one-third to a half. Season with pepper.

Tourte des Pyrénées

Many of the gâteaux that feature in the Midi-Pyrénées, especially at village markets, are prepared from a basic mix of flour, sugar, butter and eggs which, when combined in different proportions and with or without some form of leavening, produce a marvellous and distinctive array of differently textured cakes. One of these is this very authentic *tourte* found in Pyrenean villages and rarely anywhere else. Only a couple of flavour variations were ever available – the French in these parts are as conservative with their gâteau flavours as they are with wearing a beret in a colour other than black. Always *myrtille* – wild blueberry – and occasionally chocolate chip. Personally, I like to make this gâteau with glacé orange and orange blossom water; dried cranberries and glacé ginger would also be delicious.

Prep time: 15 minutes   Cooking time: 45–50 minutes   Serves: 8–10

2 cups (250 grams) flour
1 tablespoon baking powder
1¼ cups caster sugar
3 eggs, separated
½ cup milk
1 tablespoon pastis (optional but very authentic; see page 94)
2 teaspoons orange blossom water (or use vanilla essence)
¼ cup finely chopped crystallised orange slices or citrus peel
125 grams butter, melted (avoid margarine)

Preheat the oven to 180°C. Grease and line the base and sides of a 20-cm diameter fluted cake tin (also called a charlotte mould) with baking paper. Grease the baking paper.

Sift the flour, baking powder and sugar together twice to ensure it is light and well blended. Place in a large bowl and make a well in the centre.

In a clean bowl, beat the egg whites until light and fluffy. In a jug, stir together the egg yolks, milk, pastis, orange blossom water and crystallised citrus peel only until mixed. Pour into the well in the dry ingredients. Add the melted butter and beat vigorously with a wooden spoon until the batter is thick and shiny. Stir in the beaten egg whites. Pour into the prepared cake tin. If you have any sugar grains (see page 40), scatter these on top before baking.

Bake in the preheated oven for 30 minutes, then lower the temperature to 160°C and cook for a further 15–20 minutes or until a cake skewer inserted into the centre comes out clean. Leave in the tin for 10–15 minutes before turning out onto a wire rack to cool completely.

The French Pantry

The French are passionate about pastis. This aniseed-flavoured liqueur, at more than 40 per cent alcohol content, kicks like fire-water when served neat. However, when mixed at a ratio of 1 to 5 with water and maybe a touch of pomegranate syrup – often served here in beer as well – it makes for a refreshing drink that can be both warming and cooling. Prepared from oil of star anise, liquorice and herbs of Provence – although which ones exactly remains a secret – pastis can be utilised in a sweet kitchen to brighten up a frozen lemon sorbet or vanilla-bean-rich ice cream or to add charm to a rich butter cake.

mars

With the kids happier and the weather improving, I began to see the beauty in this part of rural France. No longer clouded by grey skies, an over-supply of rain and damp fog, the colour of the area, its people and lifestyle were emerging from winter hibernation.

AS PREDICTED, SPRING ARRIVED ON 1 MARCH as if someone had flicked a switch . . . but just as fast as it went on, it went off again with an avalanche of snow at the end of the first week! Then the change from winter was visible as our village and those around us, Nouilhan and Larreule, came to life.

Suddenly there were near traffic jams in the village as, wakened from deep slumber, massive tractors groaned into life, clattering out of the old timber-roofed barns close to the stone-walled farmhouses. They rumbled across the gravel courtyards and then crept cautiously through the tiny laneways to the fields jumbled around. Their ploughs cut deep furrows through the waterlogged, heavy clay soil, undisturbed throughout winter, allowing the spring sun to revitalise and nourish the earth before the April planting of the area's main crops: maize, sunflowers, wheat, rapeseed, barley, haricot beans and tobacco.

So numerous were the tractors that I wandered, steaming coffee in hand, along winter-rutted Rue Longue to watch the rural industry begin its working season. Maybe, like me, the farmers were revelling in the smell of spring after such a brutal winter, the worst in France for many decades. As the sunny days bloomed, the air in our village became opaque with dust wafting in on the southerly breeze, the result of the farmers' efforts.

Neighbours whom I had rarely seen other than when they put out the rubbish at the front gate on a Friday morning – when the wind and rain or snow kept heads down and their 'bonjour' rather faint – had windows open, bed linen out to air every morning, carpets on lines to blow away winter's trapped ashes. Aproned old ladies were assessing makeover requirements for their gardens, and in Caixon's laneways, where windows open onto the street, folk were talking unhurriedly to passers-by on bikes, or drivers who leant out of their car windows to stop for a chat, heedless of any resulting traffic issues behind them; a classic French movie scene at every turn!

The abundant fruit trees were bursting into blossom, and daffodils (called *jonquilles* here), growing wild under the laurel trees that formed informal boundaries between houses, waved softly in a gently breeze. Our back garden lawn, once waterlogged, was a carpet of daisies and dandelions. Through the months that followed, I sat regularly with Olive-Rose, making daisy chains, often late into the afternoon.

At last I could begin to resurrect my garden from its dormant winter state. Gardening is an expensive hobby there unless you plant bulbs, which are ridiculously cheap. The walled courtyard at the side of the house, which I had cleared of overgrown weeds, rye grass, straggling ugly evergreens and unloved climbing roses, was redesigned with plants galore.

PAGE 98, CLOCKWISE FROM TOP: *Caixon in spring; the Marciac market; an iconic Renault 4L Fourgonnette.*

THESE PAGES, CLOCKWISE FROM TOP LEFT: *Market day at Tillac, Gers; a poultry seller at the Vic-en-Bigorre market; bread delivery to my neighbours; a village lady catches the midday sun; cherry blossom at Au Palouque; spring lamb at Caixon.*

PAGE 103: *A corner of my garden in bloom.*

In the cooler corner, hyacinths, lily of the valley and winter roses were nestled under a straggly spruce tree. The protected south-facing wall, with its reconstructed brick well, became home to my herbs, sweet pink azaleas and old-fashioned bleeding hearts with their variegated pink and crimson flowers.

By the cool north-facing wall, which got no direct sun, I gathered up old rocks, broken roof tiles and chipped slate from lost corners of Au Palouque to create a rock garden, where purple and blue plants would cascade down the moss-covered stone.

The west-facing wall, beneficiary of much sun – and rain – sang out for decoration. I found an old semi-circle of trellis at a junkyard and painted it a bouquet of pinks and purples. Warwick, with much blaspheming, hung it on the wall as a piece of courtyard art for the jasmine and clematis to climb. Below, Mexican orange blossom, lavenders of many varieties, sweet William, variegated heathers and rosemary created a middle layer and any spaces beneath were in-filled with an array of bulbs and pink and white dianthus. From dreary and dull to fresh and creative, the courtyard of Au Palouque was taking shape as a restful haven of spring's sweet smells and colours.

Although two borders of furry-flowered and honey-scented English laurel trees sheltered Au Palouque's backyard, it was still a little early to plant vegetables. With Warwick and Graham's help, the soil was turned and home-made compost dug in before we divided the area into four plots for me to try companion planting: potatoes, peas and lettuces in one corner; beans and corn in another; tomatoes, beetroot, onions and basil filled the third quarter; and the last section featured strawberries, borage, celery and rhubarb. Alyssum and catnip were dotted here and there, the former to bring bees, the latter to deter mice of which, as our farmhouse bordered maize fields, I was expecting an invasion . . . although I did not breathe a word to Olive-Rose!

In the front yard, our cherry trees were bursting into fragrant flower. They hosted hoopoe birds, which sang loudly like drunken owls. Higher up, butternut-pumpkin-size, fluffy cottonwool cocoons exploded open, showering hundreds of processionary caterpillars onto the lawn. The resulting nose-to-tail line, 3 metres and more long, marched through the rutted lawn to find food. For Jean-Luc, whose pin-up boy is Ruud Kleinpaste, this lesson in nature turned him into a walking, talking David Attenborough for the next couple of days.

Under the towering conifers that flanked the farmhouse, I added colour with marigolds and more lavender to complement the 40-plus lavender plants now well established down the length of the driveway. Where I found space, I dug in dahlias, daisy bushes and lots of Hautes-Pyrénées wildflower seedlings in anticipation that in one year I could take Au Palouque's garden – deprived of colour and love – to new heights.

Later in the month at our local market, Vic-en-Bigorre, change was also in the air. Gone were potatoes, parsnips and pumpkin, to be succeeded by asparagus, capsicums and fancy fan-shaped, highly perfumed strawberries. Although the price was high, I indulged in strawberries and served them to the children simply dipped in crème fraîche

Buying fresh rabbit at Argelès-Gazost's Tuesday market.

and dusted with a little sifted muscovado sugar; simplicity that ensured perfection.

Gone, too, were the tables upon tables of ducks and foie gras, although as duck was the meat of choice here, a few specialist retailers remained. French spring lamb had arrived but it was expensive, so savouring this highly regarded and much written-about meat would have to wait, perhaps for a special gathering later in the spring or summer.

Plant stalls abounded with window-box selections of petunias, violas and primroses. There were also herbs: tarragon and basil – rather early, I thought, to plant – so I settled on parsley, chives and mint to add to the sage, thyme and bay already doing well in the courtyard.

The market was the closest contact I had with the locals. At the Vic market many stallholders had come to know us well. They helped me with my French, helped teach Jean-Luc and Olive-Rose how to buy their produce, gave the kids slices of cheese or *jambon* to sample, allowed them to pat live chickens and rabbits before sale, and laughed with Jean-Luc as he bartered away or interpreted for his mother.

Each week, Jean-Luc had humorous discussions with Jean-Claude at the *épicerie* stand, Ali, the fruit and vegetable man, and Thierry, the honey seller, about how our adventure was going. I admired my son as he gave French a go.

After four months my French had improved a little – *un petit peu* – to where I could greet people with confidence, ask how they were and relate date, day and time, as well as so many grams or kilograms, 'how much is that?', 'thank you', 'have a good day' and 'goodbye'. Fortunately, many locals in this area under 35–40 years of age speak a little English: the expansion of the European Community in recent decades has made an understanding of English vitally important in today's global, high-tech world.

School was rocketing along, and there were very few tears. For Jean-Luc, maths had been a big hump to overcome, and 100 per cent in a long division and multiplication test brought a smile to his face. I was relieved, as in New Zealand this subject was a struggle for him, especially with the new-format maths curriculum – but that topic is a book on its own! Here, with a one-way-only teaching philosophy, and calculations done by hand on graph paper, Jean-Luc had excelled. To me this was a lesson in not changing something that ain't broke, but I am sure the Ministry of Education in New Zealand would not see it my way!

Olive-Rose's school went on day trips to the local museum and to puppet plays, and rarely did she have any upsets at school. She was settled and had friends in the village. Interestingly, there was no ratio of parents-to-kids required to take children out, just the teacher and all her chickens. Larreule Primary, Jean-Luc's school, took advantage of the late snow season – normally all the snow is gone by March – with a couple of trips to ski fields about an hour away. All 47 kids were kitted out with skis, poles and boots at a village en route and then went onto the slopes for lessons; all courtesy of funds raised by the parents and friends at the *loto* night. Wow!

With the kids happier and the weather improving, I began to see the beauty in this part of rural France. No longer clouded by grey skies, an over-supply of rain and damp fog, the colour of the area, its people and lifestyle were emerging from winter hibernation. As a result, I felt much happier and found joy in my work again; back to cooking and writing.

The last week of March led into Easter, which brought an Easter egg hunt to a farm near us. Otherwise, little happened for this significant Christian festival. As with Christmas, the celebrations were minimal for a country that I had thought would strongly follow its Catholic heritage. There had been no talk of Lent, no Good Friday holiday and, not altogether a surprise, no hot cross buns, although I did find buttery sweet aniseed bread.

Overall, March was enjoyable. I could take my afternoon tea outside, sit in an old chair and rest my head against the riverstone walls of Au Palouque, soaking up the sun, feeling its healing warmth and looking forward to exciting months ahead with Warwick and the kids. Fishing in the river, cycling the laneways and back roads late into the evening, making daisy chains, picnicking and exploring ancient ruins, drinking coffee under leafy plane trees in the local villages all beckoned. The French village life I had hoped to experience was emerging, and it felt wonderful.

Le Pâques

In France, religion and the state have been entirely separate since the Revolution. Predominantly Roman Catholic, the French observe significant days on the religious calendar: Christmas Day, the Assumption and Easter Sunday, with Monday a public holiday for Easter Sunday. Good Friday is a standard working day.

To mark Palm Sunday and Holy Week, many *boulangeries*, market stallholders and other food businesses decorate their stores with branches of olives or bay. Easter celebrations, though, are far less commerical. Delightful displays in the windows of the *chocolaterie* (chocolate shop) or *pâtisserie* (cake shop) were the only visible sign that Easter was approaching. Splendidly decorated giant displays featured Easter characters, from bunnies to eggs, chickens and fairies. Chocolate was filled with sensuously delicious centres of praline, fruit or floral pastes, or alcoholic syrups.

The countertops at the local *boulangerie* were laden with yeast-baked sweet breads. There wasn't a hot cross bun in sight! La Gâche de Pâques (Easter bun), a brioche-like bread, is sold scented with aniseed, studded with glacé fruit or even shaped into a *couronne* (crown) and baked with an egg in the centre.

Shrove Tuesday is called Mardi Gras, or fat Tuesday, because it is the day when rich foods remaining in the pantry are eaten before the parsimonious Lent! Replacing pancakes were *beignets* (icing-sugar-coated doughnuts), *gaufres* (waffles) or crêpes, their Bourbon-vanilla-rich batters filling the fresh spring air of the village markets.

The Easter Bunny does not hop in Caixon. '*Non . . . pfft . . .* that is for the English,' said a neighbour. Instead, there are *les cloches volantes* – flying bells. According to French Easter tradition, from Thursday night all the church bells cease to ring and fly off to Rome to be blessed. In the early hours of Sunday morning, they return with Easter eggs to hide for the children, before going back to their bell towers to ring again, celebrating their return and the resurrection of Christ.

Le Vide-Grenier

Spring also means spring-cleaning. The old ways of the seasons – winter to hibernate, spring for renewal – are still part of everyday life here. 'Empty your attic' is the literal translation of the term *vide-grenier* and at these weekly events in villages all over France, for a paltry fee locals can set up a table and sell off all their household and farming junk. For us they were a combination of a car boot sale and an opportunity shop. However, the markets do not operate randomly. This is France, and even selling off *grand-mère*'s faded Tupperware requires rules and even a law!

Anyone can set up a table, but only twice a year, so if granny's Tupperware is not hot on those two weekends you're out of luck! If you set up a third time, you are regarded as undertaking unauthorised commerce, risking a heavy fine, even imprisonment.

There are, of course, forms to fill out; you must register, providing identity papers, and you must attest on your honour that you have not taken part in more than one *vide-grenier* this year and that you are only selling your family junk and not your neighbour's. A recent law change 'generously' allows you to be able to take part in *vide-greniers* outside your own commune!

I rarely missed a local *vide-grenier*, finding props for this book. With a few euros, the kids would spend ages hunting out bargains – some better than others. Often the sale would be accompanied by a French version of the fundraising sausage sizzle, the *buvette* (refreshment stall), and included *jambon*, *saucisson*, gâteaux and wine or beer.

Pascal Griffon, Le Boulanger

Bread is fundamental to French daily life; it is consumed at every meal. At breakfast, bread *is* the meal, usually baguette eaten *sans beurre* – without butter – and partnered only by espresso. For all that, the artisan *boulanger* (trained baker) is under pressure. Industrialised food-production companies provide ready-made bread mixes or preformed dough never to be pummelled, kneaded or moulded by the baker's warm, gentle hands. This goes to supermarkets, where plastic-glove-wearing shop assistants simply finish off any baking required. Mass-produced bread is, of course, cheaper and makes shopping a one-stop option, but it is also pretty much tasteless. However, in line with the burgeoning worldwide interest in the provenance of our food, in recent years the French have rediscovered their taste for products *au terroir*. That has led to a revival in buying artisan-made bread, as opposed to picking up a loaf at the *dépôt du pain*, a shop that sells precooked breads not made on the premises.

Bread's flavour is only achieved through 'love and devotion to the art of bread-making'. So states the local baker Pascal Griffon, to whose shop in the nearby village of Maubourguet we went daily to buy his hand-crafted breads.

Pascal is a *boulanger artisanal*, a title set in law. It indicates that he makes the bread sold on his premises, beginning with the flour, yeast and water through to baking. This 1998 law aims to protect the tradesman baker against industrial giants. It does not, however, cover the *viennoiseries* (croissants, tartes, gâteaux), many of which are bought in to bakers' shops frozen and ready to cook or pre-cooked, although not to Pascal's.

Pascal prepares his doughs after lunch. The differences in the recipes are a closely guarded secret, but he tells me much is about the flour, the amount of yeast and the quantity of salt. He uses only locally milled wheat, spelt and rye; too much yeast will dry out the crumb. The salt is from the Gironde and too much will affect the yeast's ability to work and its rising time; the latter is the key to flavour. The longer the dough rises, the better the flavour. Pascal leaves his dough at 12°C for a minimum of 12 hours.

In the early hours of the next morning – 3 a.m. – while the village slumbers, Pascal, in crisp baker's whites, gathers up the dough, now supple from a night of unhurried proving, and begins to knead. No scales are required, his keen eye sees and gentle hands feel the weight of each loaf. The unmistakable scent of fresh yeast-raised dough fills the air, and it is not long before loaves of bread of different shapes, sizes and styles are set to prove, some glazed, others dusted with *fleur de campagne* (coarsely milled wheat) or dried sunflower seeds.

Once the breads are baked, Pascal turns his hands to the delicate art of *pâtisserie*, making tarts decorated with seasonal fruits, choux pastry delights, croissants and the finest *pain aux raisins*, with their yeast-risen flaky pastry, rum-soaked raisins and vanilla-perfumed crème. Pascal's *pain aux raisins* is renowned throughout the wider commune and sells out quickly each day.

Religious holidays, with their traditional culinary specialities, are Pascal's busiest times. The locals want the traditional *bûche de Noël* (Christmas log) or brioche-dough-based *couronne* at Christmas and chocolate eggs, chickens, rabbits and bears for Easter.

At 7 a.m. the doors open and locals spill in to buy, and there will be a constant stream of loyal customers. Some shop twice a day for bread for *le petit déjeuner* (breakfast) and then fresh bread from a later baking for lunch or dinner. Pascal will catch up on his sleep over lunch before the routine begins again. The doors at Pascal and Fanny's *boulangerie* will be the last to close in the village, around 7.30 p.m. The long hours of preparing the most staple of French foods places the baker right at the heart of the village.

Pascal breaks open his famed Maubourguette loaf to show me that good bread must have a dry crust that makes a crusty cracking sound when torn apart. Inside, it must have dense, moist bread with an even texture and a truly delicious taste . . . so good it does not require butter; it was divine.

Duck Confit Cottage Pie

In villages where the Anglo-Saxons have become *nouveaux amis* (new friends) you often find marriages of English and French cuisine. This was one dish that cropped up pretty regularly, although I've added a Kiwi twist with orange-fleshed kumara (sweet potatoes in France) which are readily available and their taste and texture partner well with the duck. Do add the prunes; cooked with a touch of vinegar they add piquancy to the dish, lifting its richness.

Prep time: 20 minutes   Cooking time: about 40 minutes   Serves: 4–6

4–6 portions duck confit (see page 90)
1 onion, peeled and very finely chopped
2 cloves garlic, crushed, peeled and mashed to a paste with a pinch of salt
250 grams mushrooms, finely sliced or diced
2 cups gravy (best if it is home-made chicken gravy; if using a packet mix, add flavour
    with a dash of red wine or port)
1.5 kilograms orange kumara, cooked and mashed with butter and salt
½ cup grated cheese (we used Brebis [sheep's cheese], although Cheddar will be fine)

Sweet and Sour Prunes
250 grams very moist prunes
¼ cup red wine
¼ cup sugar or honey
2 tablespoons red or white vinegar
1 stick cinnamon

Preheat the oven to 180°C.
Discard the duck skin and bones and pull the meat into chunky pieces.

Cook the onion and garlic in a dash of oil in a frying-pan until softened. Add the mushrooms and stir over a moderate heat until softened.

Mix together the duck meat, onion and mushroom mixture and gravy and season with pepper or maybe some herbs of your choice. Transfer to a large ovenproof dish, pile on the kumara and scatter the cheese over.

Bake the cottage pie in the preheated oven for around 40 minutes until piping hot. Serve with sweet and sour prunes.

To make the Sweet and Sour Prunes, place all the ingredients in a saucepan. Simmer only until the sugar dissolves, and leave to stand until cool. Keep refrigerated. If using very dry prunes, you may need to add ¼ cup water.

Pain aux Raisins Slice

The evolution of the bread pudding – yes, there is one – began humbly enough. Leftover bread, soaked in milk, maybe sweetened with honey or scented with spices, was then enriched with eggs, spices and dried fruits. Further richness was added by increasing the amount of egg and milk to make a more custard-like pudding, bread was buttered – and then the culinary fashionistas took over. Brioche and croissants replaced bread, and milk was nudged sideways in place of cream. From there chocolate chips, alcohol, fruit and the like were added until the once basic use-up-leftovers pudding gained star status in the Culinary Comfort Food competition! Thus, I was delighted often to find the original slice in the *boulangeries* here, albeit made from leftover *pain aux raisins* and bread. I like these served warm and buttered – I love butter – or maybe warm with crème anglaise.

Prep time: 15 minutes Standing time: 1 hour Cooking time: 45 minutes Serves: 8

500 grams (about 6) *pain aux raisins* (best if 2–3 days old)
1 egg
1 cup milk (use full-fat milk as lite milk could curdle when mixed with alcohol)
¼ cup Armagnac or rum

Break and rub the *pain aux raisins* between your hands into small pieces and scatter into a well-greased dish. The dish should be large enough for the crumbs to be about 3 cm thick.

Beat the egg, milk and Armagnac or rum together and pour evenly over the crumbs. Press down with a spatula. There should be enough liquid to wet all the crumbs.

Stand, covered, for 1 hour. If you have any sugar grains (see page 40), scatter a few over before baking.

Preheat the oven to 180°C.

Bake in the preheated oven for 45 minutes or until set. Allow to stand for 10 minutes before cutting into squares to enjoy warm. This never lasted long in our house, but if you plan to keep it, do so in the refrigerator. You can also serve this warm with crème anglaise, a dish which featured on many *auberge* (inn) and café-bar menus under the name of Pain Perdu (toasted bread).

Financiers

Where the children went riding, at Poney Julie, there was always a joke that whoever *est tombé* – fell off – would bring the gâteau the following week. Since Jean-Luc was soon nicknamed Jean-Wayne Gofton, I was forever baking! The children in his group loved these financiers over any other goodie I took. Unlike the oval financiers we find regularly at home, in our area in France they are thin, rectangular and firm. Small and truly delicious, these are great served on a platter with fresh fruit or with a *café grand crème*.

Prep time: 15 minutes   Cooking time: 10–12 minutes   Makes: about 24

125 grams butter (preferably unsalted)
1 teaspoon almond essence
1 tablespoon Armagnac or rum (optional but adds a wonderful flavour)
⅔ cup caster sugar
1 loosely filled cup ground almonds
3 tablespoons flour
3 large egg whites at room temperature
flaked almonds for garnishing

Preheat the oven to 190°C. Lightly grease mini financier moulds and line the bases with paper. If you don't have rectangular financier moulds, use muffin tins.

Heat the butter in a saucepan until it becomes nut brown in colour. Scrape the base of the pan to ensure the sediment is included. Stir in the almond essence, and Armagnac or rum if using. Leave to cool.

In a bowl, stir together the sugar, ground almonds and flour. Add the cooled melted butter and rub through evenly; the texture will be like sand. I use my hands for this job, or you can use a fork.

Beat the egg whites until they form stiff peaks. Work into the almond mixture to make a thick batter consistency. Place tablespoonfuls into the moulds, or if using muffin tins, only sufficient to cover the base and be about ½–¾ cm thick. Scatter a few flaked almonds over.

Bake in the preheated oven for 10–12 minutes or until the edges begin to brown. Stand for a couple of minutes, then transfer to a wire rack to cool. Keep in an airtight container.

avril

The backyard boasted fig, apricot, plum, apple and pear trees. What with the warm spring sun and the bees at work, the sweet smell of spring blossom wafted in and out of our farmhouse with each gentle puff of wind.

EASTER MONDAY, UNLIKE GOOD FRIDAY, was a public holiday; it heralded April and brought with it the promise of a happy month ahead. My brother Adrian and his wife Joan were visiting from Tasmania, and another round of school holidays was due; it didn't seem like six weeks since the last ones!

My quaint courtyard garden was now in full bloom, enhanced by new chairs and tables in hot pink and faded green to match my Maison du Kiwi garden artwork (surely the Tate Modern will call?). Relaxing in it late one afternoon, cuppa in hand, I heard a hum so loud I wondered whether the village's electricity transformer outside our front gate had gone on the blink again. New to orcharding, I was taken aback to find that the hum came from hundreds of bees in Au Palouque's fruit trees. In the front garden, the branches of our three blossom-covered, gnarled old cherry trees were swaying gently under the weight and activity of the bees which, in golden sunshine, were seeking every iota of pollen and nectar.

It was the same in the backyard, which boasted fig, apricot, plum, apple and pear trees. What with the warm spring sun and the bees at work, the sweet smell of spring blossom wafted in and out of our farmhouse with each gentle puff of wind. On days when our neighbour struck up his ride-on mower, sending the bouquet of new-mown grass over on the breeze, the peaceful Pyrenean air was filled with the beguiling fragrances of countryside in the throes of spring.

Later in the week, a swarm of bees gathered on an old post and we had to call in the local beekeeper who, having ascertained that the queen was in the middle of the swarm, set up a hive nearby. The bees duly relocated and were taken to the next village. The whole process was a nature lesson for Jean-Luc and Olive-Rose, whose only honey-making experience to date had been through glass windows at a honey farm.

The vegetable garden appreciated the arrival of my brother, who has green fingers. In no time, my potager was flourishing in magazine-quality, picture-perfect rows. Baby green peas were mountaineering en masse over the willow witches' hat frames made by a local woman. As long as the kids stopped eating them straight from the garden, I was looking forward to cooking these homegrown, tiny green pearls, so highly regarded here, in a classic *petit pois à la française* (peas with cos lettuce and spring onion).

In the flower garden, which provided such joyful colour, Warwick and my brother positioned trellises and wires for the roses, clematis and jasmine to climb. Tree peonies and hollyhocks emerged from nowhere; the lavender, although still green, flourished and I eagerly waited for it to flower. The garden, once devoid of colour and happiness,

PAGE *118: The table set for afternoon tea in our courtyard.* THIS PAGE, CLOCKWISE FROM TOP LEFT: *Peonies abounded in the local gardens of Caixon; Warwick building our garden; blossoms at Au Palouque; Jean-Luc in our courtyard with the newly hung Maison du Kiwi sign.*

prospered, and I hoped that it would go on after our time here and be a joy to those who followed us at Au Palouque.

Aged sheep's cheese – Brebis (see page 202) – became a permanent feature in our larder, surprising really as my kids have never been hot on cheese. Beneath its earth-coloured, woven-textured crust is a sweet, nutty cheese, a little 'farmy', but meltingly delicious. The fresh sheep's cheese, though, is brilliant white with a highly recognisable taste. It matches well with other local gutsy-flavoured foods like Basque pepper sauce (see page 159) and, with olives, *jambon* and oregano, makes a sensational pizza (see page 159). Pizzas are a breeze to make here, as good ready-made yeast dough is available round or oblong, ready rolled, fresh or frozen.

The school term finished with a rather large test for Jean-Luc's class. The results would go towards the children's report card, which would indicate to the inspector whether the child could move on to college. The decision to move a child from primary to college is made by the inspector, not the teacher. He or she visits and looks at the work and then meets with the teacher to discuss each child's outcome. We were advised that, although Jean-Luc was of the right age to move on to college, since he was still reluctant to speak French at school he should stay at the village primary for the last six months of our stay, which was the first six months of the next school year here. We were relieved about this as the thought of having to settle him into a new school filled me with dread, especially as he was feeling happier by the day. Better still, his friends from our village would be staying on, too, so the school term ended on a higher note.

We gathered up our now six-member family and captained a six-berth *pénichette* (canal boat) down the Canal du Midi, a UNESCO World Heritage site, for seven days and nights. This trip, wandering peacefully down silent boulevards of water, was to be a highlight of our year.

With 44 locks, 15 or so up and the rest down (I lost count after a while), we drifted at a snail's pace from Negra (south of Toulouse) to Argens-Minervois (south of Carcassonne) beneath the shade of fine old plane trees, on a canal that was the most Herculean engineering and construction feat of its day. Built by Pierre Paul Riquet in 15 years (1667–1681), the 240-kilometre canal was dug by hand and joined the Atlantic to the Mediterranean. Although its use for industrial transport has long since given way to trains, cars, planes and semi-trailer trucks, Canal du Midi has become an enchanting journey for tourists. Our first two or three locks were fraught, as our lesson on steering the behemoth of a canal boat was a 10-minute chat in broken French/English. In no time, it was clear that the boys should man the boat and the girls stick to cooking and pouring the wine!

For the children, the whole experience was a blast. They jumped in and out of the boat to help with the locks, steered with their uncle's help and fished off the top deck. Off the water, there was shopping at village markets, feasting on the iconic stew cassoulet at its reputed birthplace, Castelnaudary, and exploring the treasury of villages to be found nestled behind each bend on the waterway. We cycled the picture-postcard cobbled streets of villages like Bram – built in a circular maze, around its thirteenth-century church – and explored the mediaeval *cité* of Carcassonne. Added to all this was meeting new people each night when we moored against the side of the canal or at a hamlet's tiny port.

In the second week, we went by train to Paris and, as seemed to be the way with our travels, our trip was not without the unexpected. About halfway from Caixon to the train station at Tarbes, our car squealed like a toddler throwing a tantrum, lost power and stopped dead on a dual-lane road with nowhere to pull over! Trains don't wait, but friend Chris answered our call, racing to the rescue, and we made it with less than five minutes to spare. As for the car, we grabbed our belongings, turned on the hazard lights and left it where it was – a problem for the rental company!

Too many viewings of the children's movie *Un Monstre à Paris* meant the kids had prepared a wishlist of sights including the Eiffel Tower, Notre Dame, the Louvre and more, all to be crammed into five days. Most of Europe seemed to have the same idea, although it was not peak season. Wherever we went, at Métro station, bus stop or attraction, we were confronted by a tidal wave of rude, pushy tourists in a city that, for me, had lost some of its glamour under the weight of such numbers and was grimy in parts. I longed for the Paris I had loved as a 21-year-old, but maybe to my kids' eyes, it was the same City of Lights; perhaps the rose-tinted glasses of youth fade with age, I decided. We caught the train home on May Day, a national public holiday for which even Paris closes, and traditional posies of lily of the valley were for sale on every boulevard corner to be exchanged between families and friends.

The journey on the TGV (*Train à Grande Vitesse* – high speed train), speeding through the landscape at 200 kilometres per hour for seven hours, clearly illustrated to us what an enormous and varied country France is and how lucky we were to be having this year out to experience just one small part of it.

The new term started with a triumph for Jean-Luc. Each pupil was to report on his or her *vacances* (holiday), and for the first time Jean-Luc, in well-spoken French, told his class of his holiday. So surprised was his teacher, Marie-Paule, that she stood, as did the other pupils, and gave Jean-Luc a rousing ovation. At the break he received slaps on his back and found new friends who, until this time, could not really play with him as he could not or would not speak French. We'd been told by others who had had the same experience to give it six months and he would have 'got it', and indeed he did. What a happy boy came home each night then; he had to clear this hurdle by himself and, for all the distress we had been through, I hoped this character-building exercise would help him as he grew into his teens.

CLOCKWISE FROM TOP LEFT:
*Artisan producer of cassoulet at
Castelnaudary; a world away from
home; UNESCO World Heritage
site, Canal du Midi; one of the many
lock stations on the Canal du Midi;
flower boxes appeared from spring to
late autumn; French bread – chewy,
crusty, delicious.*

Pyrénées Lamb and Mouton

The geography of the Pyrénées, from alpine mountains with lush pastures and distinctive flora to quietly undulating plains below, combined with the climate, which ranges from cold, harsh winters to glorious sun-filled summers, has been pivotal in determining the cuisine of this area. Nowhere was this more evident than with the raising of sheep – meat for the table, milk for Brebis (sheep's milk) cheese production and, in times past, wool for clothing.

Deep into the southern area of the Haute-Pyrénées is the Pays Toy, a region noted for its rugged natural beauty with high-peaked mountains and glaciers, and its spirited, hard-working shepherds who follow age-old shepherding traditions. In the picturesque alpine village of Luz-Saint-Sauveur, Chef Gérard Bor brought me to meet friend and farmer Sylvan Broueilh, who devotedly tends his 500-plus flock of Baregeoise mouton, an ancient Hautes-Pyrénées breed that he and a few dozen farmers are bringing back from the brink of extinction. Dedication to the old ways of rearing this heavy-set, long-legged, short-spiral-horned, shaggy-fleeced animal earned the breed an AOC certification (see page 224) in 2008, and recognition from the Slow Food movement for its exceptional quality.

Their diet is highly regulated, only hay and grass; no supplementing with cereal is allowed. In winter the animals are kept warm inside, avoiding the snowfalls and bitter sub-zero temperatures. Come spring, though, they face the annual transhumance, all on foot, up steep mountains to 2800–3000 metres, for here there are no roads, just well-worn tracks that have been patiently followed for hundreds of years. While the *moutons* (sheep) graze peacefully on the wild-thyme-laced pastures, Sylvan treks up once a week to check their feet and feed them salt, a journey that takes three hours each way. His passion to preserve both the ancient breed and the time-honoured shepherding practices is a credit to this mild-mannered, modest young farmer, and I can truly appreciate the effort that goes into producing such fine-tasting meat. Given, though, that there are only 5000 sheep that reach AOC standards, to taste this sublime meat you will need to visit the area, as demand far outreaches supply.

Both genders are reared for their meat, not their milk. Females are culled between two and six years or after producing five lambs, while *doublons* (castrated males) are culled between 18 and 24 months after two seasons on summer pasture. The mouton is a true *produit saisonnière* (seasonal product), only available in summer. The flesh is light burgundy in colour, with creamy white fat. It is highly perfumed, and has a sweet, concentrated yet smooth lamb flavour that is equally delicious grilled to medium-rare or served slow-cooked as *civet de mouton,* marinated for 1–3 days in Madiran wine and simmered slowly until the flesh flakes. A culinary delicacy in anyone's language.

Further to the west, still in the Pyrénées, is the village of Mauléon, home to

espadrilles (Spanish canvas shoes) manufacture, and Axuria, a cooperative of farmers who take pride in the long tradition of shepherding to produce *l'agneau de lait des Pyrénées* – Pyrénées milk-fed lamb.

Semi-retired farmers Marcel Equios and his wife welcomed me to their farm. Marcel, with his well-worn bucket hat, was a joy and his glinting eyes hinted at a mischievous nature as he thrust a baby lamb into my city-slicker arms – the never-worn look of my gumboots a give-away!

Only three local breeds are farmed for the prized and approved milk-fed lamb industry – red-headed Manech, black-headed Manech and the Basco-Béarnaise. Each summer in the transhumance, the ewes, famed for their milk which makes the most delicious Brebis cheeses, are driven to high pastures, between 1000 and 2000 metres above sea level.

In autumn, the sheep return to the valleys and the safety and warmth of sheds, and the first lambs soon follow. Not all lambs are required. About 25 per cent of females are kept and a handful of males for breeding purposes; the remaining lambs are raised for the table.

Housed indoors and fed only on mother's milk until they reach a maximum of 14 kilograms or at 45 days, the lambs are table-ready. The meat, fine-grained, has a sweet, delicate taste. This is the lamb version of veal, coming from breeds that can tolerate the terrain and weather of the region. About 350 breeders produce 50,000 lambs per year. The strict guidelines of breed, feed and age ensure the milk-fed lamb of the Pyrénées carries both Label Rouge and European Union's IGP labels (see page 224).

Highly seasonal – available only from November to July – milk-fed lamb is in high demand in Parisian restaurants, and throughout Spain; the latter takes the lion's share at Easter, when the Paschal lamb is the preferred meat for the celebratory family dinner, and also at Christmas. As in New Zealand, producers have to contend with marketing issues that arise when the preferred cuts go to the restaurant trade; legs are popular in the north, chops and cutlets in the south, and the remaining cuts go to butchers for local tables.

Les Fraises

With warmer months earlier in the year, the Aquitaine region – bordering our region to the west – produces the season's first strawberries (*les fraises*) and at least half of all France's strawberry crop. The first flush appears in late March or early April. Strawberries, like many fruit and vegetables here, are sold by variety since not all strawberries taste or look the same, and the buyer will consider which variety to buy according to its final end use.

Strawberry production here has had a chequered past. After the Second World War, French growers found it hard to compete with the abundance of cheaper and larger imported fruit from near neighbours. This changed when the French started to grow a new variety called Gariguette, choosing to compete on flavour as opposed to size and, although it wasn't an instant success, its deep red colour and sweet, intense flavour finally won the day. As the season progresses, its cousin Ciflorette appears, although for me, nothing could match the perfumed intensity and unrivalled flavour of the smaller Mara de Bois, a new cultivar developed to reflect the original woodland strawberry flavour; truly divine.

Strawberries are also available with Label Rouge certification (see page 224), which requires them to have constant attention from the producer and to be pollinated by bumblebees. Many growers thin the plant's floppy leaves to allow more spring sun to reach the fruit – laborious, but worthwhile if taste is key for producer and buyer. Further north, the Périgord strawberry growers have the benefit of having the only IGP (*Indication Géographique Protégée*, see page 224) for a strawberry in France: their label Fraise de Périgord.

As only the French could and would do, the picked strawberries – at least the ones we bought from Ali each week – were packed into *barquettes* (trays) in such a way that the point of one rested between the shoulders of those beneath, and never were there three layers as this would cause the berries beneath to collapse and crush. Strawberries never tasted so good.

Le Miel

Apiculture is a venerable and highly respected artisan trade in France. The bee, chosen by Napoleon to be the symbol of immortality and resurrection, was once indispensable, providing not only mead, honey and beeswax but also income, as its production was highly taxed. The topography of the Hautes-Pyrénées provides unique and varied vegetation for the production of *miel*. In our area, the bees' arrival heralds the change of season.

Their working calendar begins here on the plains around Caixon when sweet-scented cherry blossoms burst from wintering branches, and the buttercup-yellow fields of flowering *colza* (rapeseed) that checkerboard the area with cereal crops compete for attention with golden *tournesol* (sunflowers), producing *miel de colza* and *miel de tournesol* respectively.

Late April, May and June is the time of the transhumance, when the apiarists move hives, overnight so as not to disturb the bees from their work in sunshine hours, to the foothills of the Pyrénées. Here flowering linden and chestnut trees blossom and produce honeys at opposite ends of the spectrum. *Miel de tilleul* or lime honey from the linden tree is bright, sweet and fresh with minty notes, while *miel de châtaignier* or chestnut-tree honey is a rich caramel colour, strong-flavoured, aromatic and not too sweet. Acacia trees provide a third choice for the bees: the honey is light in flavour and a family favourite, popular with children.

As summer arrives, the bees journey upwards again to farmhouses on steep mountain slopes where *miel de bruyère*, or heather honey, is produced. The season in the Hautes-Pyrénées takes up about eight months of the year.

Since each honey has its own characteristics, buying it requires tasting and conversation with the apiarist. Single-flower honeys, like single-varietal wines, have unique characteristics, their flavours layered with nuances that come from the *terroir* and the season that nature endowed that year.

Buying honey is a serious undertaking for the French, especially if it is to be the main ingredient for the likes of a *pain d'epice* (see page 35), in which the honey flavour is critical to success. Each week we had the choice of buying from two or three honey sellers, while at the Maubourguet market, the producer from our next-door village of Nouilhan would have his stand gaily decorated with bee and honey paraphernalia. He offered tasting sticks and notes on each honey. This was routine practice at all the *marchés des Pays Hautes-Pyrénées* and rarely did I find the same producer or seller at more than two markets, there were so many artisan apiarists there.

Axoa de Veau

Veal is a very popular choice of meat in France. In the southwest, if it is to be cooked any way other than pan-fried with butter and seasoned with salt, pepper, garlic and parsley, it is more often than not found as Axoa de Veau. It's a classic dish of the Basque country, which is also home to the *piment d'Espelette* (see page 280) and Bayonne ham. This simple recipe became our favourite casserole at Au Palouque, and it is best eaten two or three days after making, when all the flavours have become friends and the meat begins to fall to pieces. It can also be made with beef, lamb or pork, and the meat may be minced rather than diced. This recipe is ideal for the crock-pot or slow cooker; about 6–7 hours on low or 3–4 on high.

Prep time: 20 minutes   Cooking time: 1½ hours   Serves: 8 (but only 6 in my maison!)

1.5 kilograms veal (shoulder is best; you need some fat to carry flavour)
1 teaspoon flaky salt (less if using finely milled)
½–1 teaspoon ground pepper (I like black but white is okay, too)
1 teaspoon *piment d'Espelette* (or use paprika and a good pinch of chilli powder)
¼–⅓ cup olive oil (not virgin oil; pick a light-flavoured one)
1 large onion, peeled and finely chopped
1–2 red capsicums, diced (deep, ripe red are essential for flavour)
8–10 large mild green chillies, deseeded and sliced
4–6 fat juicy cloves garlic, crushed, peeled and sliced
1½ cups veal or chicken stock (a chicken stock cube and water is fine)

Preheat the oven to 160°C.

Cut the meat into chunky-size pieces and with your hands massage the salt, pepper and *piment d'Espelette* into the meat – a dash of oil will help the process.

Heat half the oil in a frying-pan and cook the onion, capsicum, chilli and garlic until the vegetables have wilted. Transfer to a casserole.

Brown the veal in the remaining oil, not too much, but it should be golden brown. Add to the casserole. Browning will best be done in batches or the meat will stew and not help impart a golden colour or caramelised flavour to the cooking broth. Pour the stock into the pan, stirring over a low heat to lift any sediment from the base of the pan – this is called deglazing. Pour into the casserole and cover.

Cook in the preheated oven for about 1½ hours or until the meat is tender. This casserole requires a good 15 minutes' standing time before serving.

Rabbit with Olives

After their first meal of rabbit, the children often requested it. I did wonder if this had something to do with the competition we always held to see who would get to chop off its head and cut it up! Rabbit is lean and simple to cook, cheerfully accepts a diverse range of flavours and is delicious baked, simmered or pan-fried; in short, rabbit is undeservedly much underrated in New Zealand.

Prep time: 20 minutes Cooking time: 1¼–1½ hours Serves: 4

1 rabbit, big enough to feed four
4 slices thick-cut streaky bacon, not lean (rabbit needs fat to keep it moist)
12 shallots, peeled and left whole
1 cup dry white wine or chicken stock (a stock cube and water is fine)
1 tablespoon picked fresh thyme (try a mix of thymes to vary the flavour)
a handful of green olives, plain or marinated

Preheat the oven to 180°C.

Wash the rabbit well and remove any bits left on the inside, like kidneys. Cut the rabbit into three sections: behind the front legs and above the back legs; if the loin section is long, this can be cut crosswise into two. Cut each portion in half. Tying the pieces with string will ensure they keep a nice shape. Season well and set aside.

Cut the bacon into chunky bite-size pieces and pan-fry until the fat runs. Use a slotted spoon to transfer the bacon to a plate. Add the rabbit to the pan and brown the pieces well in the bacon fat. Transfer to a roasting dish where they have enough room to sit in one layer. Pan-fry the shallots until golden, adding a little oil if necessary. Scatter the bacon and shallots over the rabbit.

Pour the wine or stock into the pan and stir over a low heat to remove any sediment from the pan (deglazing). Pour over the rabbit, scatter the thyme over, add the olives and cover securely.

Bake in the preheated oven for 45 minutes. Remove the lid and return to the oven for about 20 minutes until the rabbit is golden and cooked. Avoid overcooking the rabbit; it will become dry and therefore tough.

Serve with buttery mashed potatoes. Any leftover rabbit can be shredded and tossed through pasta or a salad.

Crêpes with Pistachio Nut Paste

Crêpes, like no other dessert, say France to me. Indeed, *crêpes Suzette* (crêpes smothered in a silky butter, orange and Grand Marnier sauce, a 1970s culinary fashion icon) was my challenge to cook – *à la guéridon* service – at the judges' table to pass my chef's exam. Here they were cooked flavoured with rather overpowering, readily available *arôme crêpe* – a mix of almond, vanilla, orange or lemon and rum. Sweet crêpes are prepared from wheat (*farine de blé*) while savoury crêpes – *galettes* – are made from, or should contain, some buckwheat flour (*sarrasin*). Jean-Luc would buy crêpes by the half dozen, sprinkled with sugar and wrapped in foil; takeaways to delight.

Prep time: 40 minutes   Cooking time: 15 minutes   Makes: about 10

1 cup flour
3 eggs
1¼ cups milk
25 grams butter

Sift the flour into a large bowl, adding a pinch of salt if you like.

Beat the eggs and milk together and, using a whisk, begin to mix the liquid ingredients into the flour. Whisk only until smooth. If you over-beat the batter, the finished crêpes will be tough.

Melt the butter in a frying-pan and cook until it becomes nut brown in colour. Stir into the batter. Strain to remove any flour lumps and set aside for 30 minutes to allow the starch granules to rest and expand.

Spoon half-ladlefuls of batter into a lightly greased, hot frying-pan, turning the pan with a twist of the wrist so the batter quickly covers the pan base in a thin, even layer.

Cook for 1 minute – maybe a little less – until the top of the crêpe looks dry and the underside is brown, before turning or flipping. The second side will require less than a minute to brown. Transfer to a plate and repeat with the batter. As you cook the crêpes, you will find the frying-pan requires less greasing.

Pistachio Nut Paste

Pistachio nuts were available in every way possible at our village markets; they are incredibly popular in both savoury and sweet cooking. Come Easter or Christmas they are like hen's teeth to find, as they are used in stuffings for roasts, added to rich yeast baking and to fig pastes to accompany foie gras.

Prep time: 15 minutes   Makes: ¾ cup

¼ cup sugar
2 tablespoons water or lemon juice, hot
1 cup peeled pistachio nuts
1–2 drops pistachio nut essence (optional)

Stir the sugar and water or lemon juice together until the sugar dissolves. Cool.

In a food processor or blender, process the nuts until finely chopped. Add the syrup and essence and blend just until it forms a paste. Keep refrigerated.

Strawberry Tart

From spring until late in summer, the Sunday ritual in the village was to visit Pascal's *boulangerie* and buy a tart for lunch; essential if you were to be considered local! However, with children who loved to cook, we made our own.

Prep time: 1 hour   Cooking time: 20 minutes   Serves: 6

250 grams Allyson's Quick Flaky Pastry (page 264) or store-bought puff pastry, defrosted if frozen

Crème Pâtissière
2 cups milk (whole milk is undoubtedly better for flavour here)
seeds from 1 vanilla pod
1 teaspoon vanilla essence or extract (either is fine)
¼ cup flour
½ cup sugar
4-6 egg yolks (I like 6 egg yolks for both flavour and texture, but 4 will suffice)

Topping
strawberries (at least one punnet)
¼ cup red jam, sieved

Prepare the Crème Pâtissière (see below) and have it cool.

Preheat the oven to 220°C and set the rack above the centre.

Roll the pastry out large enough to cut a 25–27 cm circle. Allow to rest for 10 minutes. Place on a well-greased tray and prick pastry with a fork. Bake in the hot oven for 10 minutes until well risen and golden. Turn the pastry disc over and return it to the oven for a further 5–7 minutes or until the base is also golden. If the pastry has turned into an eiderdown of layers, press gently with your hands to flatten a little. Cool on a wire rack.

Place the pastry disc on a serving platter. Spread liberally with the Crème Pâtissière, decorate with the strawberries and glaze with the jam. Serve within an hour.

Crème Pâtissière

Put 1½ cups of the milk into a saucepan with the vanilla seeds and essence or extract and bring to the boil. Mix the remaining milk with the flour, sugar and egg yolks until smooth. Pour into the hot milk, whisking until the mixture becomes very thick. Lower the temperature, change to a wooden spoon and cook, stirring constantly, for a good 2 minutes. Transfer to a bowl and cover with plastic wrap. Cool. If refrigerated, the custard will set firmly; remove from the refrigerator a good hour before using.

m a i

The anticipation of summer saw villagers –
unseen, never mind met, until now – out
walking with dogs, pushing grandchildren in
prams or hanging out of windows chatting
to neighbours in Caixon's laneways, where
windows open onto the street.

IN MAY, EVERY ASPECT OF MY WORLD burst into colour. Despite all my years of reading about food history and the seasonal rituals of the table, at last I understood clearly our forebears' urge to celebrate spring, the season of re-birth and new hope.

With the farmers working from sunrise to dusk – 6 a.m. to 8.30 p.m. – the area came to life: it was as if a seasonal Big Ben had chimed. While fields had been ploughed and readied for this year's crops in March, the consequences of the torrential late spring downpours had created a palpable urgency to make up for lost time.

The countryside became a vibrant tapestry of colour and texture that changed daily as nature poured its warming strength into the winter-worn earth. Rapeseed exploded overnight into carpets of iridescent yellow, contrasting with the more subdued green of hectares of tightly packed broad bean plants with their beady-eyed white and black flowers. Verdant stretches of young wheat abutted russet-coloured fields where baby maize and potato shoots could just be seen. So luminous were the yellow rapeseed flowers that some days, under a perfect blue cloudless sky, your eyes would almost hurt when you looked at them without sunglasses.

In every major village or small town, including our local towns of Vic-en-Bigorre and Maubourguet, council workers in reflective clothing, cigarettes in hands and complete with berets, were everywhere. They tidied up the rotten remains of winter's weeds from the ditches, sprayed mildew, scrubbed signposts and planted boxes of brightly coloured flowers, including the popular geranium in a rainbow of colours. The generously planted tubs, square or round, plastic, metal or terracotta, were everywhere, creating the classic postcard French village look. My favourites were the ones hung under the weathered pastel blue shutters of windows in government buildings. I reflected that at home, these costly public floral displays would be vandalised within a short time of being established. Here, they are admired and no one would damage such public property without risking the village's opprobrium!

In Caixon, vegetable gardens were being tended, weeds removed, and there was an unmistakably floral scent in the air from the profusion of roses and peonies that were in full bloom. On the evening breeze, after the day's heat, when we would all bike through the laneways, the scent was captivating, and in the colours in many gardens I could see a Monet painting awaiting artist and easel.

PAGE 144: Summer crops at a Larreule farm.

CLOCKWISE FROM TOP LEFT: Blossoming trees at Cauterets; broad beans for the pot; spring in the Bigorre Valley; plenty of time to chat – no-one ever seemed in a rush in this part of the world; come spring, farmhouses burst into colour; flowering hanging baskets were abundant at all of the spring and summer markets.

The number of stalls at the Vic-en-Bigorre market doubled; not that there was much room for that to happen, I thought, but somehow tables were shuffled to enable everyone, from the radishes-only seller to the bigger stallholders, to fit in.

Juicy strawberries were in abundance, sold in large single-layer trays, perfect for presentation. New potatoes, too, had appeared, making a welcome change from mashed spuds. The IGP Île de Ré potatoes were a real treat and I boiled them in their skins and served them slathered with a boutique butter made from unpasteurised cream, and a generous seasoning of the sweet, crunchy crystals of *fleur de sel* (salt) from Salies-de-Béarn.

Locals clutched bags full of freshly picked, unshelled *petits pois* (peas) and broad beans and I joined the queue to buy some. I shelled the beans and gently cooked them in stock, then crushed them and mixed them with mint and thyme from the garden before serving as an *apéritif* in baby pastry shells on a bed of a whipped cream cheese called *fromage fouetté*, adding chopped local *jambon* to some. The peas – or what remained after the kids had shelled them – were savoured au naturel with butter; sweet, firm-textured *petits pois* are far too precious to bury under a superfluity of flavours!

My small potager garden was having a mixed season, the wet spring having wrought havoc. An odd flower appeared here and there on the heritage Rouge des Flandres and Corne de Gatte salad potato varieties, the onions and beetroot were looking good, the broccoli was being picked, and the green beans were climbing well. The lettuces were coming along and the parsley had gone mad; I could see we would be eating *le persil* for the next while! My baby tomatoes and capsicums, sadly, were ruined and I needed new plants. The pear, plum and apple trees had tiny buds of nascent fruit, promising a good crop.

I adored fresh-cut flowers so I planted sweet William, carnations, geraniums and more to complement the Mexican orange blossom and flourishing roses.

Nearby, the Gers region village of Saint-Sever-de-Rustan holds an annual flower fête in the grounds of the twelfth-century abbey that sits proudly on the banks of the Arros River. I wandered under the cooling shade of stately old trees through a fairground of all things garden-related, and joined in singing with the Mayor and his ragtag choir.

I left my kids free to entertain themselves, knowing that they would only seek me out if they needed a drink and that if they crossed the line, a local would let them know! Between watching a knot of village women spin and knit angora rabbit and lambs' wool and taking an interest in a basket weaver's craft, they rode endlessly and for free in a festively decorated, restored carriage drawn by a handsome chestnut draught horse through the Lilliputian laneways of the village – kids' heaven!

The anticipation of summer saw villagers – unseen, never mind met, until now – out walking with dogs, pushing grandchildren in prams or hanging out of windows chatting to neighbours in Caixon's laneways, where windows open onto the street. At the all-weather picnic table and chairs, set beneath leafy plane trees outside Au Palouque's walls, oldies of the village gathered in the late morning or early evening to chat. They arrived on walkers, bicycles or with walking stick . . . and there was always a dog.

Out of the blue, in the dying days of the month, unexpected storms struck. So wild were the rain and winds that I feared our old house would crumble, and the kids were wide-awake with fear as raging winds blew. Cherries hailed down from one of the fully laden trees, and for the fourth time since our arrival the village was flooded in. Fields of young maize lay awash in shallow lakes of water; near-dry rapeseed was sodden. Accustomed to the vicissitudes of their existence, farmers grimaced sourly as they talked of 40 per cent crop loss; there would be little profit this year and, in rural France, this was a disaster. Shutters once again closed against the weather and as we turned the calendar to June we all prayed for the return of the sunshine.

Les Violettes

For many of us the scent of violets is redolent of times past, invoking memories of grandmothers or even great-grandmothers; it is the perfume of another age. This tiny ancient flower – it is mentioned in Greek mythology – became the pre-eminent scent of the European courts, especially France in the 1700s, to the extent that commercial production was required to supply the demands of the wealthy. While countries competed to find new varieties, it was the double-flowered Violette de Toulouse, with its intense perfume, discovered in the early 1800s, that fanned the craze for the 'flower of faithfulness'.

In the early 1900s – the violet's heyday – Toulouse (capital of our region) had 600 registered growers. Records show that in 1909 they produced 600,000 bouquets, each with anywhere between 25 and 200 flowers. By 1950 Toulouse had established a code as to how the violet should be presented: 20 violets and one red rose in a bouquet for a lady whose heart had been won; 5000 to be used as a cushion for the funeral of a cardinal. It was an enormous industry, providing employment for generations of families.

From the late 1940s the violet began to suffer from disease, floods and the move to the production of less time-consuming flowers; low-growing violets were labour-intensive. In the 1990s chemists at Toulouse University developed a way to isolate the diseases and pests that lived in the soil and greatly affected production, establishing a system of growing the plants in pots away from the soil on waist-high tables, greatly reducing the labour component of production.

Thus, the flower of faithfulness – true to its name – was reborn and every part of the flower is now used. Bouquets grace flower stalls at markets, celebrating the arrival of spring. Crushed flowers are crystallised – now the best-known product of the industry. With their irregular shape, intense colour and fine sugar coating, crystallised violets sparkle like cut amethysts, decorating meringues, gâteaux and *viennoiseries* (pastries) in every *boulangerie*. The leaves, which produce 95 per cent pure violet extract, are used in the cosmetic and fragrance industries and the food industry, where the extract flavours everything from custards to macaroons, as well as savoury foods such as mustards – a popular partner to the glorious duck of Gascony. The stems are ingeniously distilled to make a popular violet liqueur.

Serge Dubertrand, Le Boucher

As French manners dictate, Irene, our guide in all things French, introduced me to the local *boucher* (butcher), Serge Dubertrand, and his charming wife Josette in the first week of our arrival. Merely to turn up would not be appropriate, especially given my meagre French. A beaming smile from a mountain of a man whose large hands reflect a lifetime of working with raw, cold meat – and probably the odd rugby game – welcomes us to what would become a year-long friendship. There is plenty of laughter as I point to my body to describe the parts of the animal I wish to buy, embarrassing my children and causing much mirth among the other customers.

Serge, like so many people of his age in this area, followed his father into the trade. The *boucherie* (butchery), established in 1937, has always been a family affair. Although Serge, who took over the shop in 1975, passed the daily running of the business on to his son Christophe in 2007, he still lives at the back of the business and works daily; retirement is clearly not a consideration.

The weekly routine has changed little, with early starts and a six-day week, which includes taking the *boucherie* truck to the market on a Tuesday and travelling to outlying villages on the other days of the week to cater to customers who are unable to come into town for whatever reason.

Serge routinely attends the market sales because he likes to see the animals on the hoof before purchase, and it's a chance to shake hands with the farmers, to garner news of the industry and be aware of any issues. Monday is market day for pork and veal, Tuesday for beef, Thursday for sheep. An average weekly purchase is 600 kilograms of beef, two veal carcasses, five pigs and six or seven sheep, all reared locally. Serge will know the farmers from whom he has made the purchase, and each carcass comes with a certificate stating the farm of provenance, including a photo of the animal. These certificates are prominently displayed in the shop because the customer wants to know the origin of the meat. This need to understand the provenance of their food sets the French cook apart from us in many ways. Where we would flinch at a photograph of the animal, taken before slaughter and now displayed in Flintstone-size pieces in the chiller cabinet, for the French housewife it is essential.

Beef is bought by breed. In this region, the Blonde d'Aquitaine spends time on lush grass, coupled with many hours under cover away from harsh winters and, with a relaxed feeding pattern, produces beef with a fine texture and well-rounded flavour.

Lamb under three months of age is pretty much a speciality. Here, meat of 14 months of age is considered lamb. *Mouton* (what we know as mutton) is the norm. Between two and three years old, it has a strong flavour and is best served, as tradition in this area dictates, well cooked.

The carcasses are delivered whole, au naturel – there's no muslin wrapping here –

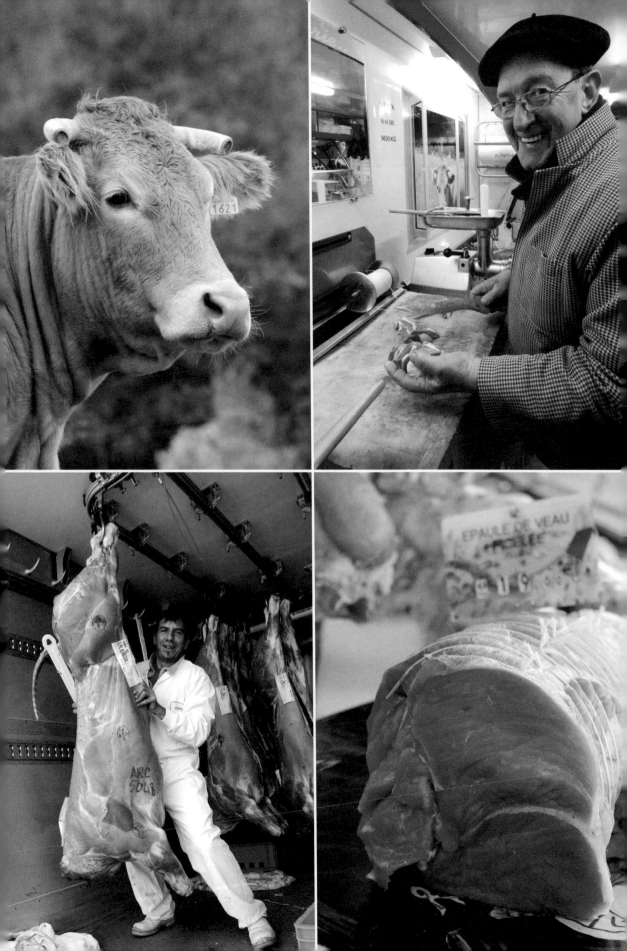

then left to hang and, if required, age before being prepared for presentation. The chiller cabinet looks nothing like those at home. There are no black polystyrene trays, no parsley to 'pretty-up' the scene, no pre-cut, pre-crumbed or pre-wrapped anything. You come to the butcher to buy meat, and that is what he offers.

Large, colourful platters hold cuts of meat that can weigh up to 20 or 30 kilograms. You do not need to know your chuck from your cross-cut, your cutlet from your chop, or your sirloin from your Scotch. The French butcher their animals totally differently to Anglo-Saxons. Here you tell the butcher what you are going to cook and he will advise what is best, depending on what he has available. Often my theatrical displays of showing where I wanted the meat cuts from was met with 'Non, non, Allyson. This is better', and so I spent the year buying what I was told to.

Once Maubourguet supported five butchers, but today as times change only two *boucheries* remain. Serge has kept up with the need to be innovative, employing a chef who prepares a selection of home-cooked meals, much appreciated by the older customer who lives alone and by busy working families. *Boeuf en daube* (beef in red wine), cooked pigs' trotters, jellied tripe, *boudin noir maison* (black pudding), *pâté en croûte* (pâté in a pastry crust), *pâté Provençal* (pork and herb pâté), *confit du canard* (duck confit), *Parmentier de poulet* (potato-topped chicken pie), *flan maison* (baked custard), *rillettes d'or* and *rillettes de campagne* (potted meats) and more; all recipes come from Serge's family.

Salted meats – *poitrine fumé* (smoked belly pork), *saucisson sec* (dried sausage, including *béret Bigourdan*) – are a speciality of his right-hand man, Yannick. Also on offer are wines, locally made canned duck products such as foie gras and *confit du canard* and cooked Tarbais beans.

In a world where pre-cut meats sit characterless on supermarket shelves, complete with absorbent pad lest we see that meat cries blood when it is sliced, corseted and unable to breathe under industrial-thickness plastic wrap, the time I had with Serge and his team was, for a cook, refreshing.

Sides of lamb were broken down into legs, middle sections and shoulders. All on the bone, they would be presented to me, then cut to my requirements, trimmed, deboned or frenched if required. Shoulders of beef, deboned and rolled into a 20-plus kilogram log of meat, would be sliced to my preferred thickness to grill. Enormous whole rumps sat majestically, and they and slabs of *joue du beouf* (beef cheek) would be cut to size. *Jarret du veau* (veal shanks) would be sawn on request for osso bucco. Pork spareribs were sold by the length and only cut into single ribs as required and never pre-marinated. Fresh *saucissons* (sausages), sold by the length, kept company with hearts, kidneys, liver, tripe and pig's head for brawn.

Each request was deftly prepared with great attention to the customer regardless of the size of purchase, be it one slice or ten. If the queue went out the door, as it often did, *tant pis* (too bad)! Each customer was offered personal, unhurried service.

I watched this skilful butcher performing to his most ardent critic, the French housewife, all the while chatting, gossiping and flirting; an all-day concert, just different acts with each '*bonjour*' and '*au revoir*'.

This has been a way of life for Serge's family for three-quarters of a century. Taking it all in, I felt a tinge of sadness that we no longer buy our meat like this, not only for the butcher but also for the farmer, whose competence to raise animals for the table and to be truly appreciated for his expertise is pretty much absent in our lifestyle, lost to speed and price.

For Serge, his family and his team, the dedication to his trade has brought a lifetime of enjoyable work and deep friendships. I appreciate and understand the importance of the local butcher to the villages of France: may it never change.

Gascon Sausage Rolls

In an attempt to bring a little New Zealand flavour into our life, occasionally I made these sausage rolls, giving them a French twist by using duck sausages. The children would not normally eat duck sausage, but liked these and, being Kiwi kids, had tomato sauce with them. Now and again, we would indulge in the luxury of a hollandaise sauce, scented with either herbs from the garden or orange rind, all of which are perfect with duck.

Prep time: 45 minutes   Cooking time: 25 minutes   Makes: 12

400 gram block frozen puff pastry, defrosted
1 onion, peeled and finely chopped
4 cloves garlic, crushed, peeled and mashed to a paste with a pinch of salt
500 grams duck sausages (if not available try lamb, beef or pork, but they should be
    very chunky in texture)
1–2 well-packed tablespoons chopped fresh herbs (whatever you have to hand)
chopped pistachios (if desired)
beaten egg or milk to glaze the pastry

Roll the pastry out on a lightly floured benchtop – too much flour will make the pastry tough – until it is about 30 cm x 20 cm. Rest.

While the pastry rests, cook the onion and garlic in a very generous spoonful of butter until the onion is well cooked. Cool.

Squeeze the duck meat from the sausage skins, discarding the skins. Mix the meat with the onion mixture and herbs and season well with salt and pepper. Add a few chopped pistachios if you have any to hand, but they are not essential.

Cut the pastry in half lengthwise. Divide the meat mixture in half and spoon it evenly down the length of the two pastry pieces. Roll the pastry over to enclose the filling. It will seal better if brushed with a little egg glaze or milk between the layers.

Brush the top of the rolls with egg glaze or milk and, using a wetted knife, cut into 5 or 6 pieces. Mark the tops with a few shallow knife cuts and transfer to a well-greased baking tray. If time permits, refrigerate the sausage rolls for 30 minutes, which will ensure the pastry cooks evenly. The sausage rolls can also be frozen at this time for later use; defrost before cooking.

Preheat the oven to 200°C and place the oven rack above the centre. Puff pastry needs a hot blast to get the layers rising; if the oven is too cool, the layers will melt together rather than rise and flake and the end result will often be raw and chewy.

Bake in the preheated oven for 20–25 minutes or until golden.

Basque Jambon and Apricot Pizza

Over time, Basque flavours have infiltrated this area of France. The Basque region lies in the southeast corner of the Bay of Biscay and comprises a little of France, but mainly Spain. We always knew when we had crossed into the borderless Basque region as the road signs would be in Euskara (the Basque language), French and/or Spanish. At a local market in San Sebastián, I picked up a pepper sauce, which we made into a base for Basque-inspired dishes like chicken or lamb casseroles and pizzas; this combination is a flavoursome blend of the Hautes-Pyrénées and the Pays Basque.

Prep time: 15 minutes   Cooking time: 20 minutes   Serves: 5–6

2 medium pizza bases (see The French Pantry overleaf)
½ cup Basque Pepper Sauce (see recipe below)
150–200 grams fresh sheep or goat's cheese, sliced
6 very thin slices *jambon*, halved
10–12 juicy dried apricots, torn into halves
a few good-quality, moist black olives
½ cup grated Brebis (sheep's) cheese (or use Edam)

Preheat the oven to 200°C and set the rack just above the centre.

Roll out the pizza bases and use to line a greased 35 cm x 25 cm (approximately) oven tray. Spread the Basque Pepper Sauce on top and arrange the sliced cheese evenly over the sauce. Twist the *jambon* slices and sit them in among the cheese with the apricots and olives. Scatter the grated cheese over.

Bake for 18–20 minutes. Serve with a few fresh chives or oregano scattered on top.

Basque Pepper Sauce

Prep time: 15 minutes   Cooking time: 45 minutes   Makes: about 3 cups

1 kilogram red capsicums, halved and deseeded
100 grams (about 6) large mild red chillis, deseeded to keep the heat down
6 large, fat, juicy cloves garlic, crushed, peeled and sliced
½ cup olive oil (one with a good flavour)
2 teaspoons flaky salt or 1 teaspoon finely milled salt
½ teaspoon pepper (black is better than white here)

Continued over the page

½ teaspoon dried thyme

1 large tomato, deseeded

¼ cup chopped fresh parsley (any type, as it will be puréed)

Place the capsicums on a foil-lined baking tray and brush with oil. Grill under a high heat until just blackened, cool and peel.

In a large saucepan, cook the chilli and garlic in half the olive oil until the garlic has softened but not coloured. Add the peeled capsicums and remaining ingredients (except parsley) and simmer gently for 20–30 minutes, stirring regularly until the capsicums have completely softened. Add the parsley and cook for a minute or so.

Purée in a blender or with a stick blender until the sauce is very smooth. It will be thicker than a tomato sauce. If you wish to thin, add boiling hot water. Bottle in hot, dry, sterilised jars. Seal when cold and keep refrigerated.

The French Pantry

Pizza bases here come as pre-made dough – round or oblong – and all that is required of the cook is to unroll the dough onto a greased tray, add toppings and cook. Light in texture and not too thick, it is a great way to buy pizza bases. Use whatever base you prefer – home-made dough or pre-bought pizza bases.

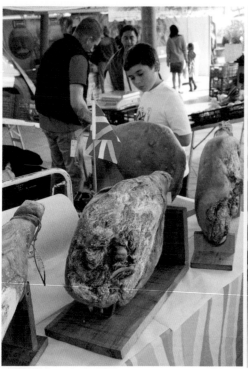

Roasted Garlic Chicken with Bean Stew

Good-quality Label Rouge chickens came at a price but were delicious. These birds, with their golden skin and grapefruit-coloured flesh – gained from eating locally grown maize – cooked beautifully to have succulent well-flavoured flesh and crispy skin. Rose garlic (see page 180), roasted in oil until the flesh of each clove melted to a velvety, honey-coloured paste, mixed with the salt-crystal-flecked butter, made a sensational paste with which to season the chicken.

Prep time: 40 minutes once garlic roasted   Cooking time: 50 minutes   Serves: 4–6

1 bulb garlic
125 grams butter (non-dairy-lovers could use ¼ cup olive oil)
4–6 chicken leg and thigh portions
a few fresh sage leaves
4–6 thick cut slices pancetta or bacon

Preheat the oven to 190°C. Drizzle the garlic bulb with a little oil and wrap in foil.

Bake in the preheated oven for 35–45 minutes until soft. Cool, halve, squeeze out the cooked flesh and mix with the butter (or oil).

Lift the skin from each chicken portion and spread a generous amount of garlic paste between the skin and the meat. Spread the remainder on top. Place a sage leaf and a slice of bacon on top of each portion and season with pepper.

Bake in the preheated 190°C oven for 40 minutes or until cooked. Serve with Tarbais Bean Stew or potatoes, cooked to your choosing, and a green vegetable.

Tarbais Bean Stew

Prep time: 15 minutes   Cooking time: 15–20 minutes   Serves: 4–6

2–3 stalks celery, finely sliced
1 leek (onion is too strong here), white part only, finely sliced
1 green chilli, deseeded and sliced
¼ cup olive oil
3 cups cooked haricot beans (I used Tarbais beans)
3–4 cups chicken stock (1–2 stock cubes and water is fine)

Cook the celery, leek and chilli in the olive oil until softened. Add the beans and chicken stock and simmer for around 15 minutes until the beans are well flavoured.

Season with salt and pepper and, if wished, add herbs of your choice; sage is good with beans as it helps with the flatulence that beans are notorious for creating!

Slow-roasted Garlic

This is a stunning dish to serve to friends as a nibble or entrée. When cooked well, the garlic is unexpectedly smooth and mellow.

Prep time: 5 minutes   Cooking time: 1½ hours   Serves: allow 1 bulb per person

garlic bulbs (fresh if early in the season, dried if later)
sprigs of dried or fresh thyme
olive oil (your finest)

Preheat the oven to 160°C.

Sit clean bulbs of garlic on the sprigs of thyme in a deep, lidded dish, and season with pepper.

Pour your finest olive oil over the garlic until it comes half to two-thirds of the way up the sides of the knuckly bulbs. Cover.

Bake in the preheated oven for about 1½ hours, or until a skewer can easily be inserted into the centre of the garlic. Remove from the oven and cool in the oil.

Serve the bulbs with chewy sourdough bread cut into thick doorstep-like slices. Cut the garlic in half horizontally, squeeze out the pulp, mix with a little of the oil and spread on the bread. Accompany with chopped fresh tomatoes and parsley.

juin

Cherries, in Europe, are the first of the tree-grown spring fruit crops and, like no other fruit, signal the end of winter. I bottled, poached, baked, jammed and made cherry tarts until we could eat no more!

MY DAD ALWAYS TOLD ME that when the first moon of the lunar cycle comes in on its back, it will be sunny – the saucer-shaped moon will hold the water. However, if it is on its side, the rain will spill out and it will be a wet month. June's moon, hidden behind ferocious storm clouds, was obviously upright!

The pilgrim town of Lourdes, to the southwest of us, sank under a tsunami of melting snow and rain that, in its rush down the Gave de Pau, gathered trees, road and house debris and poured into the lower depths of the city. It wrought havoc on the famed religious site and much of the lower town – the grotto became an underwater cave and the underground cathedral's bench-seating for 20,000 was floating in a lake. Deaths were recorded and emergency crews escorted inhabitants from several villages to safety. Many villages were cut off for the next few months, so severe was the damage.

Our village fared not much better, and yet again we were flooded in. I felt like I was living in a groove on a stuck record. People canoed in the streets and crops were under water once more. The oldies in our village spoke of gloomy skies until the end of the month! Even the hardy Brits wondered where the sun they had chased to southwest France to enjoy during retirement had gone, and retreated indoors. Food prices soared at the market as seasonal foods became scarce.

I had planned to walk the transhumance. Villages closer to the mountain's foothills celebrate the annual trek of moving animals up to cooler, higher ground for the summer season with fêtes and fairs. Families can join in on this journey, so long as you are prepared to start at 3 a.m. and hike for a good 14 hours or more! Not surprisingly, these events were cancelled due to the weather. Then, come mid-June, the sun appeared and with a vengeance. The long days of sunshine that we had dreamed of experiencing arrived, and overnight the winter wet evaporated. The change was extraordinary.

The fruit on one of the three cherry trees that provide peaceful shade to Au Palouque's south-facing front wall was a rotting mess, and the birds were having a merry, boozy feast on the fermenting fruit. The remaining two trees were heavily laden with later-ripening, Tom Thumb-size cherries in shades of burgundy, crimson and deep scarlet. Cherries, in Europe, are the first of the tree-grown spring fruit crops and, like no other fruit, signal the end of winter; this year, their late arrival was doubly welcomed.

We collected 60 kilograms and then called it quits, thinking the birds would doubtless like to party on a bit longer. I bottled, poached, baked, jammed and made cherry tarts until we could eat no more!

PAGE 168: *Unseasonal floods in Caixon again!*

THESE PAGES, CLOCKWISE FROM LEFT: *A chestnut bay takes shade in the June sun; pastel-blue shutters, closed from mid-morning to late afternoon; the doors of Abbaye Notre-Dame de l'Espérance were always open, welcoming visitors; Au Palouque's cherries.*

In the backyard, pear, apple and some of the plum trees survived the wet. The tiny fruit buds of last month were growing nicely and I saw the need to stock up quickly on more preserving jars. The collective hum of the bees on the flowering quince tree – its fruit would not ripen until autumn – could be heard from my bedroom on the second storey.

My own garden had ups and downs; clearly I did not have green fingers! The night-life did not help; each morning I awoke to more holes, half eaten plants, and gnawed areas on the solid wood edging. Visions of the movie *Over the Hedge* ran through my mind – me in night-dress against the night-life! Suffice to say that anything growing underground – potatoes, onions, beetroot and carrots – was doing well, but anything above ground – lettuces, broccoli – was fighting a losing battle, although we managed a decent enough harvest for the kids to think we did well, and that was just fine by me!

My next-door neighbour, Madame Vignaux (no relation to our Mayor), who only ever ventured out once the temperature got close to 30°C, had much more luck with her garden. She grew only a few things, but her flower baskets and pots that now appeared in every crumbling hole of her stone farmhouse were a joy.

The window boxes of family homes appeared overnight and the markets were awash with ready-planted window boxes and hanging baskets, many featuring the ubiquitous geraniums in hues of *rouge* (red) and *rose* (pink). Caixon, I noticed as I walked Olive-Rose to school each morning, was being painted pretty every day as new flower arrangements found their way onto windowsills, fences, balconies and stone walls.

On the farms, *colza* seed pods were being harvested and their stems baled; wheat and barley were bowing their heads by the end of the month. Famers sporting berets still spoke of being a whole month behind the normal schedule, but accepted they were not in charge of Mother Nature. Poppies grew at random in empty pastures, wheat and barley fields and I recalled John McCrae's poem 'In Flanders fields the poppies blow / Between the crosses, row on row'. A moment for reflection, especially as the Resistance worked courageously in this area during the Second World War.

Roads leading in and out of villages here are flanked on either side by aged plane trees, which in winter look like half-rotting carcasses – especially those that are pollarded earlier in the winter. But now, their long branches, trained in their youth to bend over the roads, made elegant, serene archways.

All in all, Caixon and the surrounding area was bursting into life. Families and schools were gearing up for exams and the forthcoming long *vacances*.

With winter heading south of the equator, many friends and family decided to come north and from mid June the visitor bookings in my diary for the next three months made us look like the unofficial Down Under Consulate for Southwest France. Visitors gave us the opportunity to show off this relatively unknown area of the country, which by now we were falling in love with. Combining Warwick's love of the classic Tour de France bike routes, such as the Col du Tourmalet and Col d'Aspin, and mine of food, many day trips took us into the mountains where specialities like Gâteau à la Broche (see page 282)

and Tourte des Pyrénées (see page 93), *fromage de brebis* (sheep's cheese), *jambon noir de Bigorre* (cured ham from Bigorre, see page 182) and various *saucissons secs* (dried sausages) could be found . . . even donkey *saucissons secs*!

Less than an hour's drive south from Caixon leads from flat, intensely farmed fields and classic riverstone farmhouse villages to picturesque, chocolate-box alpine villages with large-stoned, high-pitched, slate-roofed houses that look just like the drawings in my favourite childhood book *Heidi*.

Many of the villages in the lower reaches of the Pyrénées are spa towns, which in the mid-1800s were the places to take the cool air and warm mineral waters and recuperate from the trials of life. Later in the nineteenth century, spa towns fell out of favour, especially with the travelling Brits, as Queen Victoria led a fashion to enjoy the seaside. Today, with ski runs to tempt in winter and sensational alpine walks to trek from spring to the first snow, these towns have rejuvenated themselves. Towns like Argelès-Gazost, Bagnères-de-Bigorre, Luz-Saint-Saveur, Cauterets and Gavarnie have designer spas with beauty and therapeutic treatment options to invigorate the most weary tourist . . . at designer prices, of course!

There were pretty boutiques in cobblestoned side streets offering exquisite goods in striking Bigorre and Gascon designs to tempt you to part with euros. Delightful café-bars spilled onto pavements, above which apartment awnings often had a touch of fading grandeur about them, adding to the overall charm. So, too, did the stunningly well-manicured, centrally located gardens with splendid flowerbeds and often a carousel. Classically European in design, with ornately carved and painted Hans Christian Andersen scenes, traditional flying horses or Chitty Chitty Bang Bang-like cars, these carousels enchanted young and old alike. Olive-Rose and Jean-Luc would ride on them for ages, laughing with delight – leaving us free to people-watch.

There was a palpable peacefulness in these villages; life went on as it always had, with no rushing; there was time to chat to friends, and most things could wait until tomorrow. My 20-plus years as a food editor and food presenter have been dominated by deadlines, often urgent ones. In a counselling session for understanding family life, when I felt there was a need for us both to learn how to raise children – deal with tantrums, learn to say 'no' and so on – the counsellor said 'self-employment is not conducive to family life'. Reflecting on this – and life – over a coffee in a village town miles from home, I had to concede that he had a point.

The last few days of June were enjoyed taking in the end-of-school-year events. Jean-Luc's school had cultural dancing: the kids had learned regional Occitan dances. They and their parents dressed up as their favourite characters. I mistook a very good Astérix for Robin Hood, winning no brownie points. Jean-Luc, who refuses ever to dress up, decided being a Richie McCaw lookalike was as good as he was going to try. My job was to take a cake and I took my favourite Casa Luna spice cake. Before I left I had requests for the recipe. It's interesting that many French women think British women are born with a baking gene; very few French women bake in their homes; instead they buy their sweet baked goods from the *boulangerie* or *pâtisserie*. However, they did ask for my recipe and I just hope that my shaky French translation was accurate.

Olive-Rose's school visited a farm, where they all got to feed pigs and chickens and have a horse ride. An afternoon tea on the last day included a play, a few songs, cordial and Tourte des Pyrénées, chippies and a few lollies. That was it; make your own fun and laughter. Simple stuff, and on that happy ending away we rode on our bikes into summer.

PAGE 175: *Summer's warmth after spring rain ensured the village gardens were alive with colour.*
THESE PAGES, CLOCKWISE FROM TOP LEFT: *The sleepy village of Saint-Justin in summer; flower boxes on the bridge colour up Maubourguet's St Martin église; dried cereal crops in Laurreule await harvest; shopping at the many summer markets was a joy; Abbaye Notre-Dame de l'Espérance; farmhouse at the nearby village of Tarasteix, now sparsely populated.*

Les Oignons

In France, to be considered half good at cooking, before you so much as even consider preparation of a dish you must know your onions, for the selection is not a one-colour-brown-suits-all one.

Onions – red, white, brown and yellow – are a member of the lily family and their close relations include spring onions, leeks, shallots, garlic and chives, all of which have their own unique flavour: hence the French housewife gives her choice very careful consideration. At the Familial Auberge in Vic-en-Bigorre, I relished a meal of baby French mussels drenched in a shallot-thickened cream sauce. The shallots, cooked to melting tenderness, were so wonderfully sweet that I could not help but mop up every last soupçon of sauce.

Brown onions are an essential in the store cupboard both for their long keeping ability and the underlying well-rounded sweet flavour they give dishes when cooked. Raw, they are too strong and will act as a kissing repellent, for sure! Red onions, also called Spanish or Bermuda onions, are mild and sweet, ideal to eat raw; when cooked they will brown quickly, gaining an intense caramel flavour. Mild-flavoured white onions can be served raw, although they perform best when cooked in butter until they collapse.

The nearby Hautes-Pyrénées village of Trébons is home to *l'oignon Trébons* production. This elongated onion is referred to as *l'oignon quatre saisons*, and production covers two-thirds of the year. Premiering in May, it is fresh and sweet. By August the Trébons is *demi-sec* (half dried). Then, in autumn, the bulbs are replanted to be disinterred in November, when they are used to prepare a sweet onion confit – a classic partner for the region's foie gras.

Doux des Cévennes onions, produced in the south/central region and with their own AOC (see page 224), come to market from May to September. The mild flesh, hidden beneath satin-paper wrapping, was truly delicious raw or softened in butter, but it was not a long keeper.

Shallots are sweet, without the acidity of onions, making them ideal for mild-flavoured dishes or sauces. In the southwest, the *échalote grise* (grey shallot) reigns supreme and is a favourite with *chefs de cuisine*. Its blushed amethyst flesh is well protected beneath several layers of heavy-duty grey, papery skin. Although really time-consuming to peel, it was worth the effort; its taste is unique, pungent, sweet and addictive. The more common *échalotes rouges* (red shallots) are a good all-rounder.

L'Ail

The presentation of *l'ail* (garlic) for sale more resembles floral displays than food here in the southwest; and as each variety arrives to market, the displays become even more elaborate, for the French kitchen does not operate without *l'ail*.

Pearlescent paper-white garlic is the mildest of the three varieties – white, pink and violet. L'Ail Blanc de Lomagne from Gascony has its own IGP (see page 224) – garlic production is serious business, and it's important for local growers to be able to identify regionally grown product.

Violet garlic, so named because of its gift-wrapping-like skin – vibrant cream with violet streaks – arrives to market in plaited tresses, threaded wreaths or bound as a bouquet. It has a well-rounded medium-to-strong flavour, perfect for all styles of cooking. The most famous, L'Ail Violet de Cadours, also has its own AOC (see page 224).

Rose garlic's baby pink-blushed paper skin is the ultimate camouflage for this hot and gutsy-tasting garlic. Elegantly displayed in rows, each one top and tailing the one below, they look like a gift box of princess-perfect whirligigs. L'Ail Rose de Lautrec – grown in and near Lautrec in the Midi-Pyrénées – was awarded a Label Rouge and IGP status in 1996.

Early-season garlic has a milder flavour and arrives with firm, light-green stalks and damp skin. As the season progresses and the garlic dries, its flavour becomes stronger. Cooks here will consider what the final flavour of the dish should be and choose the variety of garlic accordingly.

The easiest way to add garlic to recipes so that its flavour permeates evenly is: on a garlic-only chopping board, crush the clove(s) with the flat blade of a cook's knife to break the core end, which makes peeling, the next step, so much easier. Chop coarsely, then sprinkle with salt and use the tip of the cook's knife to mash the salt into the garlic to form a paste.

Le Porc Noir de Bigorre

Caixon lies in the Bigorre, a valley area that begins on the northern slopes of the Pic du Midi and falls away to the flatlands of Tarbes – our main town – and the plains below. Many villages here include the word Bigorre in their name, defining exactly where they are, like Vic-en-Bigorre, our market town and Bagnères-de-Bigorre, a romantic spa town in the Pyrénées foothills.

The area is home to the *porc noir de Bigorre* – an ancient breed of black pig (records go back to Roman times) related to the Spanish Iberian pig. The magnificently preserved twelfth-century Cistercian l'Abbaye de l'Escaladieu, which nestles in the Vallée de l'Arros in the Hautes-Pyrénées, was once a major stop for pilgrims on the Chemin de St Jacques (St James Way) during the Middle Ages. The monks at the abbey tended herds of up to 2000 black pigs.

In later centuries, until the Second World War after which so much changed in France, every village family in this area kept a black pig. Each morning, a swineherd appointed by the village would collect all the pigs and take them to forage in the acorn-rich forests of the area, returning them at the end of the day; the swineherd's payment was food, no money changing hands.

In the past, the southwest was famed for its pig farms. The nearby village of Trie-sur-Baïse hosted what was then the largest pig market in France, and an annual pig festival, but with the arrival of industrialisation after the Second World War, the pork industry moved to the north of France.

Now, after years of decline, the black pig of Bigorre is undergoing a renaissance, slowly returning from the brink of extinction after the 1970s, when the pig industry turned its attention to intensive farming methods and to breeds that grew faster and leaner. The black pig grows at half the speed and has 10–15 per cent less lean meat than commercial types; the fat is essential for bringing flavour and character to the meat.

In 1981, a consortium implemented a programme to save the breed's genetic heritage through the last two boars and 30 or so sows – all the animals that remained. Once that was achieved, the challenge for the following decades has been to make the black pig commercially viable in face of competition from the crème de la crème *jamón ibérico* (Ibérico ham), cured from the black Iberian pig. That the challenge is being met is evident through growing markets; Japan, the major importer, takes 40 per cent of the legs.

Sophie Deffis, breeder of the handsome Noire d'Astarac Bigorre (Gascon black chicken, see page 56), also breeds Noir de Bigorre pigs, and on my visit the sows were busy feeding three-week-old piglets. To 'oohs' and 'aahs' from my suburban-raised rascals, Sophie gathered up a couple of the cutest piglets for them to cuddle, and I am not sure who squealed the most – the piglets, or my two with delight.

The rules for rearing this patrician breed are many. The farms must be in the

Bigorre, with a maximum stocking rate of 25 pigs per hectare. The animals must be of pure Gascon origin and must be fed only on rye, barley, chestnuts and acorns; 70 per cent of the cereals must be non-GMO. The sows will have two litters per year and, while suckling their young, must be led to pasture every day. Once weaned, the young pigs are reared in sheds on straw bedding or under shelters in meadows, where the unique flora of the Pyrénées plays a crucial role in the final flavour. The pigs must be fattened in the meadows and woods for at least six months before slaughter, at around 12–14 months and a noteworthy 160 kilograms.

For the pork to become the prized Jambon Noir de Bigorre (Noir de Bigorre ham), the legs will be cured using salt from the salt marshes of the Adour Basin. They are then left for 10–16 weeks, allowing the salt to work its way slowly through the flesh, developing the flavour and turning the well-marbled, flesh-pink meat into the blushing crimson colour of the end product. From here the hams are hung at room temperature for 10 months, with the lean areas covered with a flour and pork-fat paste to ensure even drying. For the final 10 months, the hams move to open-windowed rooms to dry and age. This last step is critical in achieving the Jambon Noir de Bigorre's exceptional flavour. Here the hams will be subject to the 'Foehn effect', a wind pattern unique to the foothills of the central Pyrénées. The Foehn is a warm, dry wind which blows through the area every three to four days, alternating with a damp Atlantic wind. After a minimum of 20 months, the legs of pork will be ready for sale (now weighing 5–7 kilograms, from 9–13 kilograms when fresh) at 40 euros plus per kilogram. A kilogram should last for six months because it should be carved very thin, like tissue paper.

Each wafer is a slice of heaven, its silky-smooth texture and sweet, intense flavour worth every cent to savour; this *jambon* and the artisans, who are so devoted to its production from farm to table, will be an enduring memory of my time here.

Shallot Confit

For a long time I have enjoyed the precise, informative and straightforward food writing on all things French by Anne Willan, who has had a very distinguished career in the United States and France. In her book *The Country Cooking of France*, I came across a recipe for confit of *échalote grise* (grey shallot), which is addictive. Few young people we met cooked with these pungent, thick-skinned shallots, preferring the easier-to-peel red ones. However, the oldies loved the gutsy flavour of the grey shallots and were very happy to invest time in peeling them; the reward was in the eating. I made a number of variations on this confit when grey shallots were available, including using honey in place of sugar or adding herbs from Au Palouque's garden.

Prep time: 45 minutes   Cooking time: about 40 minutes   Makes: 2 x 300 gram pots

1 kilogram shallots, peeled
3 tablespoons unsalted butter (salted butter will burn)
2 tablespoons sugar or honey
1 teaspoon chopped fresh thyme or oregano (optional)

Cut any larger shallots in half lengthwise to ensure that all the bulbs are roughly the same size, essential to ensure even cooking. Bulbs that are not well cooked will cause the confit to go off later.

Melt the butter in a large frying-pan and scatter the shallots on top. They need to be in one layer. Cover with foil, pressing the foil down on top of the shallots and tucking it around the edges.

Cook over the lowest heat for 20–25 minutes; the shallots should be softened and gorgeously brown. Sprinkle the sugar or honey over, stir gently and then cover again with the foil and cook, still on the lowest heat, for a further 8–10 minutes, until the shallots have caramelised. Scatter over and fold in the herbs, if using.

Pack into dry, sterilised jars and keep refrigerated. Serve at room temperature with grilled or roasted meats.

Duck Salad with Shallot Confit Dressing

No matter where we enjoyed a salad, the ingredients were few and simple, allowing the ingredients to sing in harmony, not fight to be heard. When the sun shone, we grilled or barbecued marinated duck breasts, served them sliced in a simple salad and enjoyed them with bread and wine in the courtyard. The dressing always began with shallot confit with 'things' added to it, whatever was in the cupboard, so while this is my suggestion below, do experiment.

Prep time: 40 minutes   Cooking time: 10 minutes   Serves: 4

2 oranges
2 tablespoons olive oil
1 tablespoon Armagnac or brandy
1 teaspoon minced fresh ginger
½ teaspoon salt
½ teaspoon coarsely ground pepper (white, black or green)
2–3 duck breasts

Salad
salad leaves for four (preferably small-leaved, such as lamb's lettuce)
2 avocados

Shallot Confit Dressing
½ cup Shallot Confit (see recipe page 185)
¼–⅓ cup mild-flavoured olive oil
drizzle of balsamic or wine vinegar

Grate the rind from one orange and mix with the olive oil, Armagnac or brandy, ginger, salt and pepper in a sealable plastic bag.

Make several deep cuts in the skin of each duck breast, deep enough to see the meat, and add the breasts to the marinade. Seal and massage well. Set aside for 30 minutes to marinate, preferably at room temperature. This is much harder to achieve in the refrigerator and you would need to allow at least 2 hours.

Cut the white pith from the grated orange and segment the flesh. Toss with the salad greens of your choice – keep the selection simple – and add slices of avocado.

Grate the rind and squeeze the juice from the remaining orange and set aside.

Heat a frying-pan and place the duck into the hot pan, skin-side down. Have the pan hot, but not scorching. Cook the breast for about 3–4 minutes and turn. If at this stage the frying-pan is a pool of duck fat, tip most of it out (but keep it for roasting potatoes!). Cook the second side for 2–3 minutes. Transfer to a plate to rest. The cooking time will depend on the thickness of the duck breast; you need the meat to be rare to medium-rare. Overcooked duck breast is dry and chewy.

Into the pan, add the reserved orange rind and juice, shallot confit, olive oil and vinegar and warm through; do not boil or it will wilt the salad leaves in a flash. Slice the duck and arrange on a plate, top with a generous spoonful of the Shallot Confit Dressing and arrange a handful of salad on top.

Note to Cooks

The duck cooking time will vary. If, when you slice the duck, you find it too rare, quickly pan-fry the slices for a moment. Always cook duck meat from room temperature. Cooking the second side will take a little less time, as there is no fat layer for the heat to have to penetrate.

Farmhouse Vanilla Pound Cake

Tea and cake in France comprised either goodies from the *boulangerie* or an elegant butter cake, whose quality and finesse came from the simplicity of the ingredients and the making. Prepared by using the weight of four eggs as the 'base' measure, from which the weight of all the remaining ingredients are calculated, a good pound cake will only be as good as the quality of the ingredients used to make it. I varied this recipe all year, adding glacé fruits, citrus rinds or the various international vanillas sold at the village *marchés*. This cake will benefit from a few days' grace before cutting; vanilla and butter make better friends if given time to become acquainted – especially in this recipe.

Prep time: 15 minutes   Cooking time: 50–60 minutes   Makes: 1 cake

250 grams finest butter, preferably unsalted, softened but not melted
1 cup caster sugar
2 teaspoons vanilla extract or essence (use the best you have)
1 teaspoon vanilla powder or vanilla paste (if available)
4 eggs at room temperature
1⅔ cups flour
1 teaspoon baking powder
1 vanilla pod (optional)

Glaze
2 tablespoons each caster sugar and boiling water

Preheat the oven to 180°C. Grease and line the base and sides of a 25 cm x 10 cm loaf tin.

In a warm bowl, beat the butter, sugar and vanillas with an electric beater until the mixture is very, very light and fluffy: it should look like well-whipped cream. Beat the eggs together and add a little at a time, beating into the creamed mixture, which should be very voluminous. If the eggs are cold or are added too fast, the mixture will split – if this happens, remedy the situation by beating in a spoonful of the measured flour.

Sift the flour and baking powder together at least twice and preferably three times, as the baking powder has to be evenly incorporated into the flour. Fold the flour into the creamed mixture. Pile into the prepared loaf tin and sit the vanilla pod on top if using.

Bake for 50–60 minutes or until a cake skewer inserted into the centre comes out clean. Stir the glaze ingredients together until the sugar dissolves. Brush the hot cake with glaze. Stand for 5 minutes before turning out onto a rack to cool. Wrap when cold. Serve sliced.

The French Pantry
Eggs from the refrigerator can easily be warmed up by sitting them in their shells in a jug of warm water for 2–3 minutes.

juillet

Here in the Hautes-Pyrénées, there is beauty everywhere – no tourists, just adorable locals, great food, sensational scenery, picture-postcard villages, markets, village fêtes; a France rarely featured in tourist brochures.

THE CHANGE FROM JUNE TO JULY went far beyond the weather. If I had ever thought for one moment that this inland, mountain-bordered, rural region could never offer the excitement of Van Gogh's Provence or a summer holiday on the Med, then I was much mistaken.

Here in the Hautes-Pyrénées we were beginning to truly appreciate the qualities of a largely unknown France, rarely featured in tourist brochures or magazines. Undiscovered by the trendy set, this is the France of Elizabeth David. There is beauty everywhere – no tourists, just adorable locals, great food, sensational scenery, picture-postcard villages, markets, village fêtes and more. There's a profound sense of pride, love and celebration of heritage – and we were racing to keep up now that the two-month *vacances* were upon us.

Our guides in all things French, Graham and Irene, had advised that there would not be enough days to see and do everything while the holidays were on. Heeding their advice, we took a week's break to catch some sun, surf and *pintxos* – fancy tapas – in San Sebastián. Like a movie set, this seaside city had become our favourite place to holiday, with its ancient alleyways, spectacular trading history on the port side and glamorous boulevards filled with label boutiques on the other – both within cooee of a pounding surf beach. The kids were amazed that in less than two hours we were in a different country with completely different customs.

Back at home, markets were finally bursting with the summer produce that had been delayed by bad weather, and I could scarcely keep away. The *marchés de pays* (country markets) of the Hautes-Pyrénées that operate within this region keep a centuries-old tradition going in even the tiniest village, so I could go to a market every day of the week. However, I had three favourites: Vic-en-Bigorre, on a Saturday, is the main one in our area, Tuesday is a smaller one at Maubourguet and on Wednesday the historic *bastide* town of Marciac has a colourful outdoor market in the village square. Marciac's famous August Jazz Festival has helped gain the town Grand Site of the Midi-Pyrénées status.

I went to all three – different stallholders, different supplies. *Les échalotes grises* are available at Marciac. Agen prunes, meaty, soft and sweet, are at Maubourguet. Natalie sells the most sensational *pain du passion* only on Saturdays at Vic, while a group of likely lads from Britain make cracker British bangers, which the children loved, and they are at two of the markets. My weekly routine included visits to all three and, naturally, a *café grand crème* or a *plat du jour* (dish of the day).

The markets are not just about cuisine; there's gossip to catch up on, too! As one

PAGE 192: *Musician playing chimes.*
THIS PAGE, CLOCKWISE FROM TOP LEFT: *Actor dressed as a mediaeval peasant, in dyed blue cloth, at the Bleu de Pastel fête; cows with their horns regally decorated with pastel; jester at work; Jean-Luc dressed in chainmail at the mediaeval fête.*

neighbour's mother explained, if she is not at the market by ten in the morning, there's an ambulance at her house by eleven; her friends worried that all is not well!

July and August are fête season . . . village fêtes, cultural, historical, musical fêtes – name it and, in summer, France will have a fête to celebrate it. We kicked off with a trip to the east of Toulouse, to the magnificent Château de Loubens-Lauragais, hidden amidst rolling fields of wheat, sun-bathing in over-30-degree temperatures. Behind the walls of the moat-surrounded château, mediaeval aficionados hold the Bleu de Pastel fête. Jean-Luc and Olive-Rose were taken back in time, as crafts-people dressed in costumes in various shades of blue took centre stage. Troubadours played and sang, donkeys plodded – with much coaxing – pulling cartloads of kids, swordsmen recreated battles, dyers coloured cloth, potters assisted kids to make coat-of-arms plaques. We savoured a mediaeval-style lunch of boiled eggs, chicken nibbles and fruit, wrapped in a cloth that doubled as a napkin, sitting on a sun-drenched lawn beneath old trees, while we watched actors on a makeshift stage play out the history of the plant *le pastel* (see page 198) in a funny and action-packed play . . . in short, a marvellous day.

Next was an important mediaeval festival in our own area at the Château de Montaner, built in the fourteenth century by Gaston Fébus for protection during the Hundred Years War. The weekend's events, in glorious surroundings such as only old Europe can provide, under a cloudless blue sky, enthralled Olive-Rose and Jean-Luc, who found that when history came to life beyond the pages of a book, it was a subject full of wonder to explore and find out more about.

Actors and artisans proficient in mediaeval crafts like poetry, falconry, sword fighting, ironwork, archery, cookery, pottery, music, dancing and more, travel France setting up camp and performing at recognised fêtes. Their clothing and makeshift workshops are all hand-made, as they would have been hundreds of years ago. Swordsmen in layers of padded calico-like fabric, with hand-made iron helmets and chainmail, looked – and smelled – like real knights at arms must have done. The cook, covered top to toe with a food-encrusted apron (no running water in those days), stirred a potage mix in a cast-iron stew-pot hung over an open fire. The minstrels may have looked like jesters, but their captivating music, played on reproduction mediaeval instruments, had even the reserved French dancing at the lunch tables.

The day ended with the re-enactment of a battle, complete with siege catapults, sword fighting and jousting – simply magic, especially when you're 10!

Our Caixon fête was lower key. Mussels and *frites* (chips), barbecued *saucissons* and salad were on the menu, as the townsfolk gathered outside the Mairie for a weekend of non-stop partying that included the Caixon International Pétanque Championship, hotly contested by the older men.

There was also the doorknock appeal, which is not quite what you might think. The young folk of the village dress in a theme (this year was in honour of the new-born Prince George, so we had royal lookalikes) and go around on the back of a trailer, making a lot

of noise and asking for money. It's an annual ritual left over from the days of national conscription. The boys who were going on a compulsory year of military service would knock on the doors to say goodbye to the villagers who, in turn, would give them a donation to help them on their way; nowadays the money goes to helping run the village.

At Labatut-Rivière, a delightful village by the River Adour, we joined Graham and Irene at their village fête. As I asked the boys on the barbecue to smile for a photo, I couldn't help smiling to myself at the simplicity of the scene. Here, off a country lane by a nondescript river, 200 adults and 30 or so children gathered to eat or just to have an *apéro* and party.

The form was: take your own plate, cutlery and drinks, but buy a ticket for food. Two slices of Charentais melon and a slice of thick *jambon* were dished out by the girls, while the blokes cooked beefsteaks (blue or rare and don't complain, this is France) on barbecues made from half oil drums. There was a half baguette per person and a scoop of salad; unfussy, unpretentious and delicious. No sign of any dour, fun-spoiling Health and Safety inspectors here; or if they were, they were partying, too! Dessert of profiteroles and apple slice, cut from monster-size baking trays, preceded an outstanding fireworks display that, for a village of 300 people, made some of our events at home look amateurish. We did not see the kids all night. They were busy riding bikes in the dark with new friends, jumping themselves silly on the bouncy castle or making up hide-and-seek games. This was proving to be a summer of amazing memories.

The following weekend we did it all again at Maubourguet; how many fêtes can you have?! Each village has one feature for which its fête is noted: Labatut, fireworks; Caixon, pétanque; Maubourguet, art. At this last the main street with its archway of plane trees is closed for the week to let local bars and cafés set up tables on the roadway to serve the revellers. Some 100 artists set up their easels on the sidewalk and paint; their work is auctioned the next day for charity. On opening night, there are a few speeches by the Mayor and local dignitaries, a complimentary pastis, then Maubourguet erupts into a street party for all and sundry. I can't imagine this happening at home. July was a month of non-stop joy.

Le Pastel

The leaf of the plant *Isatis tinctoria*, known as woad in Britain or *pastel* in Europe, produces a natural blue dye, its unique, gentle hue strongly associated with the France of the past. Pastel's history is long and fascinating, and for those who could grow and prepare the blue dye, wealth came in sackloads.

Pastel flourished from the twelfth century throughout Europe, but it was in the mid-1400s that the pastel barons rose. Their financial rewards for producing what became the noble colour in France built the city of Toulouse and many large châteaux nearby. However, wars and a rival – indigo – led to pastel's demise, and by 1800 it was sidelined in the museum – literally. Pastel artisan Denise Siméon-Lambert, owner of company Bleu de Pastel de Lectoure, retrieved seeds from the Conservateur des Plantes Médicinales et Tinctoriales museum near Paris to bring this intriguing plant back to life. She has had a 21-year love affair with pastel, gathering many mediaeval and Renaissance enthusiasts along the way, culminating in the festival, which spreads the word about pastel far and wide.

Dominique Bouchait, MOF, Le Fromager

Each week at the Vic market, I would join the queue to buy our weekly cheese from *fromager* (cheesemaker) Dominique Bouchait, MOF. His cheese shop on wheels arrived very early each Saturday, laden with the finest French and imported cheeses, butters and crèmes, fresh pasta, eggs and yoghurts.

Although the market did not really get underway until eight o'clock, the girls, Jennifer and Corinne, who manned the Vic *marché*, needed a full hour to ready themselves before the onslaught of regulars. The queue was often so long I'd leave one or both kids in line while I sorted out the remaining shopping.

Dominique is television material, strikingly handsome with the physique of a rugby prop, passionate about the *patrimoine* (heritage) of rural southwest France, yet keenly aware of the need to operate in an international marketplace. He is outspoken and knowledgeable on the cheeses of the Pyrénées, so often overshadowed by the media favourites like Brie and Camembert.

As a youngster growing up near Toulouse, Dominique dreamed of becoming an ornithologist. His only experience of rural life was regular visits to his grandparents, who were *fromagers* in Montréjeau, Haute-Garonne, the department next to ours. In time, his parents came to assist the ageing generation in their small cheese-only business. They established a Petit Casino (think Four Square) and added a wider selection of European cheeses and *épicerie* (grocery) items to grow the business. Dominique, by now a carefree young man, came to help his parents for a year, stayed for 27 and has no plans to leave; he fell in love with the area and the cheese.

In the early days, most market-based *fromagers* were both producers and sellers, or they bought from the other artisan cheesemaker and on-sold at the market. Dominique realised that if the business was to grow, he needed to complement his wide international cheese selection – over 200 – with his own brand of unique local cheeses, and so Mont Royal was born. He approached selected producers of Pyrénées cheeses to produce exclusively for Mont Royal. Dominique takes different styles, in cow's and sheep's milk, then matures the cheeses in his own cellars where they are washed, turned and/or salted as required.

Dominique's best-known creation is Napoléon, an aged sheep's milk cheese. Mont Royal receives the young cheese at three days and, as if it was a young child, monitors its progress every day. Its unique character is achieved by washing with *saumure* (salt brine) two to three times per week, checking it daily for humidity, temperature and flora on the crust and allowing it to mature for a minimum of 12 to 24 months, when it is called Napoléon Reserve. It has produced a wow factor in the competitive cheese industry; it has been served to Barack Obama and at the French President's table, and is now the leading cheese sold in the Pyrénées.

Complementing this are other Mont Royal creations using milk produced only in the Pyrénées: Regalis, a ewe's milk blue cheese, is a new style for this area (think Roquefort but sweeter); Petit Mignon, a small white-rind goat's cheese, delicious served warm; La Pipoune, a Pyrenean version of Reblochon but produced with ewe's milk; and Bethmale, a traditional pressed raw cow's milk cheese.

Creating and selling consistently fine cheese takes more than one man. Dominique demands high standards in animal husbandry; well-cared-for animals produce high-quality milk. He doesn't much mind if cheese is made from pasteurised milk or not, 'for both,' says Dominique, 'make good cheese, just different, but poor-quality milk, pasteurised or not, will make bad cheese'.

He cares for his customers – he knows they have bought cheese all their lives and will want to see, taste and ask about the products. Dominique insists that his staff sit exams before he lets them loose to sell. Four years ago he himself undertook the gruelling MOF (Meilleurs Ouvriers de France – Best Craftsmen in France) exams. These awards, created in 1924, recognise exceptional skill and knowledge in the artisan's trade – in Dominique's case *fromager*. Holders of the MOF are eligible to wear the distinguishing red, white and blue bands on their uniforms, and it is awarded for life.

Six days a week, eight full-time staff are awake before the birds. They begin work at 4.30 a.m. to drive Mont Royal's seven vans around the Pyrénées, attending over 30 markets anything from 14 to 120 kilometres from base. Some 500 kilograms of cheese per day is sold, on average in 100-gram pieces; each is presented to the customer for approval before purchase.

At our Vic market, Jennifer and Corinne were patient with not just my poor *patois*, but also my regular dilly-dallying about what to buy. I felt like Gretel tempted by the gingerbread and lolly house, except it was cheese. Peering through the glass front, I was bewildered by names and styles from stinkingly pungent to nut-like sweetness, smooth and creamy to crumbly and dry, white and fresh to tawny and aged. Being able to taste them, with samples for the kids, too, was a culinary adventure par excellence each week.

If only we could buy cheese like this at home and not have to put up with pre-packaged, plastic-wrapped yellow blobs thrown into sale bins, how much more wonderful the world of cheese would become for us and our families!

Fromage au Lait de Brebis

The Pyrénées Mountains create a natural border between France and Spain, although most of the range lies on the Spanish side; it begins and ends on two coasts.

The area on the Atlantic boundary is dominated by Basque culture. High rainfall sweeps in from the coast to create lush pasture in isolated valleys. Eastwards, the Béarn has softer, rolling inland pastures, although the mountains tower over it. Our inland Gascon area, with its summits of Pic du Midi and Pic du Jer, features remote villages in hidden valleys. Catalan-speaking Spanish, warm dry days and the culture of the sun heavily influence the Mediterranean end of the Pyrénées. Across this region of southern France, the stunning Pyrénées dominate the terrain that is instrumental in keeping the village industry of making Brebis or sheep's milk cheese (*fromage au lait de Brebis*) alive and thriving.

Large dairy companies have not ventured into these remote valleys, leaving hundreds of small-scale farmers able to tend small flocks of 100–200 sheep to make *fromage fermier*, cheese made by the farmer, using traditional practices – unpasteurised milk, hand-cutting of the curds. The small flocks, often hand-milked, produce only enough milk daily to make two or three wheels of cheese weighing 4–5 kilograms. The labour-intensive nature of the cottage industry has kept families together for generations.

Such cheeses are available from the farm gate or at the weekly *marchés* in their local villages or nearby. The farmer or his family will set up a simple table with cheeses on display, photos of their farm, the animals and sometimes accompanying handwritten signs. The somewhat rustic appearance of the wheels belies the satisfying quality of the cheese beneath the weathered rind.

Other unpasteurised Brebis cheeses are available. The best known is the Ossau-Iraty, one of only two ewe's milk cheeses holding an AOC (see page 224); the other is Roquefort. Ossau-Iraty has been produced for centuries in Ossau in the Béarn Valley and Iraty in the Pays Basque. The thick beige rind shields a firm ivory cheese, creamy yet with crystals on the tongue; these are formed during the *affinage* or ageing period.

There are also some recent newcomers. High up in the mountains to our east, Benedictine monks at l'Abbaye Notre-Dame de Belloc developed their own label in the 1960s, the location ensuring it is truly seasonal. Produced only in winter, the cheese is dusted with paprika before ageing. Our *fromager* Dominique's Napoléon (see page 199), now very popular, has expanded the category considerably. The pasteurised P'tit Basque, developed by a French dairy giant and prepared from pasteurised sheep's milk, is exported, helping to increase awareness of the category.

I rarely cooked with Brebis, partly because it was expensive but mainly because I wanted to savour the flavour to best advantage, preferring to follow tradition, which dictates the cheese be sliced and eaten with knife and fork along with *confit de cerises* (thick whole cherry jam). Served this way it is also known as 'farmer's dessert'.

Duck and Pork Rillettes

Rillettes are traditionally made by a *charcutier* (pork butcher) and sold at the *charcuterie*, a term that literally means 'cooked pork meat'. In past centuries, *charcuteries* were only allowed to sell cooked pork and raw pork fat, although at Lent they could sell salted fish. As time passed, the art of *charcuterie* has gone from bourgeois to haute cuisine and with the advent of supermarkets and global manufacturing, the skilled *charcutier* is hard to find – beyond the local butcher or duck seller who also sells cooked meat dishes. We had to travel to bigger villages or even cities to find one. Rillettes are like a coarse paste, prepared from meats, usually pork or at least some pork with duck, rabbit or other gutsy-flavoured meat. Where there are pigs you will always find rillettes, although the most common rillettes we bought were duck. I have mixed the two. This recipe makes a good amount. As well as serving rillettes with baguette, I like to serve it atop a pizza, giving this classic dish a makeover.

Prep time: 15 minutes   Cooking time: 4 hours   Serves: 10–12

1.5 kilogram duck
1 kilogram pork shank
2 onions, peeled and chopped
a good handful of fresh thyme (or half the amount if using dried)
1½ tablespoons coarse salt or 2 teaspoons finely milled salt
2 cups water
2 teaspoons *quatre épices* (see The French Pantry opposite)
2 teaspoons coarsely ground pepper (black or white)

If you are short of a large stockpot or saucepan, ask the butcher to cut the duck into pieces and saw the pork bone in half. You can probably do the duck by yourself, but the pork bone is best left to the professionals.

Put all the ingredients into a large saucepan and bring to the boil. Cover, and lower the heat so that the liquid will just murmur – this is an ideal occasion for a simmer mat. Leave to simmer for 4 hours; the meat has to fall completely off the bone. (If you're not planning to be nearby for this long, once it has come to the boil, transfer to a crock-pot and cook on high for 8–9 hours.)

Strain off the liquid and set it aside so that the fat rises to the top. When the meat is cool enough to handle, pull the meat off the bones and discard the bones and skin.

Using forks, shred the meat into long, string-like pieces and place in a bowl. Skim the fat off the reserved liquid and set aside. Add sufficient liquid, about 1 cup, to make a soft mixture that holds together. Transfer to a terrine-type dish and flatten with the back of a spoon. Refrigerate until firm. Once the meat is firm, pour the reserved fat on top. Depending on the amount of fat you have collected, you may need to melt additional duck or pork fat. Keep refrigerated. Under a layer of fat the rillettes will keep well for 10 days to 2 weeks. Spread·on crusty firm baguette, or serve with salad, atop a baked potato or on a pizza.

The French Pantry

Quatre épices, or four spice, is a classic French mix often used to season meat for making terrines, pâtés and smallgoods, especially those with a pork base. Mix together 1½ tablespoons ground white pepper, 2½ teaspoons grated nutmeg, 2 teaspoons ground ginger and ½ teaspoon ground cloves. Keep in an airtight container.

Basque Beef and Capsicum Tart

Boeuf haché (minced beef) was never pre-minced sitting in the window at Serge's; it had to be requested. Window space was the butcher's canvas, a place to display his skills like a Renaissance still-life: evenly sliced T-bone steaks or lamb loin chops were arranged in perfect layers, rolled sides of beef skilfully tied, dressed legs of French lamb, hand-made *saucissons*, prepared *paupiettes* (seasoned minced forcemeat enclosed in thinly sliced meat), all perfectly presented to entice the customer – but not mince. On request, completely fat-free pieces of meat would be weighed and ground and, if required, shaped into burgers while you waited. It had to be fresh, and knowing from what the mince was prepared is a French housewife's prerogative.

Prep time: 30 minutes   Cooking time: 30 minutes   Serves: 6

300 grams shortcrust pastry

Filling
1 onion, peeled and diced (brown or red is fine)
6 large cloves garlic, crushed, peeled and mashed to a paste
¼–⅓ cup olive oil
350 grams minced beef (find the leanest you can)
100–125 grams chorizo sausage, diced (a hot spicy chorizo will add good flavour)
1½–2 teaspoons *piment d'Espelette* or paprika
1 large ripe tomato, deseeded and diced
1 cup grated cheese (we used Brebis here, but Edam or even Colby will be fine)
3 red capsicums, grilled lightly and finely sliced (peel only if wished)
½ cup juicy black olives, either plain or marinated

Preheat the oven to 190°C and set the rack in the middle.

Roll the pastry out and line the base and sides of a 25 cm flan tin. Line with baking paper and baking-blind material. Bake blind for 12–15 minutes until the pastry edges are beginning to brown. Remove the baking-blind material and return to the oven to cook until well done. This step is essential.

Increase the oven temperature to 200–220°C.

Cook the onion and garlic in half the oil in a frying-pan until well softened; set aside. Heat the remaining oil, and brown the mince and chorizo sausage well. Return the onion and garlic to the pan with the *piment d'Espelette* and the diced tomato. Cover and simmer for 15 minutes. The mixture has to be thick, so if it is wet, simmer without the lid until the excess liquid evaporates.

Scatter most of the cheese over the base of the pastry shell. Spread over the mince, and scatter over the capsicum, olives and remaining cheese.

Return to the 200–220°C oven for 12–15 minutes until the tart is hot.

Cherry Jam

The arrival of cherries is greeted here with immense joy. Their appearance heralds the change of seasons, consigning winter and its miseries to memory. Once they're here, the race is on to poach, preserve and pickle. Cherry jam is essential for accompanying the Brebis cheeses.

Prep time: about an hour   Cooking time: about an hour   Makes: 6 x 300 gram jars

1.8 kilograms cherries, stoned
½ cup lemon juice (not Meyer lemons; choose thick-skinned lemons)
1.4 kilograms sugar

Place the cherries in a preserving pan. Get out your mallet or hammer and, with a solid chopping board as a base, crack open a good handful of cherry stones. Gather up the tiny, pale cream-coloured kernels on the inside – they are packed with almond-flavouring qualities – and add to the cherries with the lemon juice.

Bring very slowly to the boil, stirring the fruit with a wooden spoon to ensure it does not stick to the bottom. This takes time; don't rush it by turning up the heat, as all the fruit needs to soften well.

Once the fruit is well softened, add the sugar, stirring until it has all dissolved. Now increase the heat and bring to a rapid boil for 20 minutes. Cherries have next to no pectin – hence the added lemon juice – so they will give a soft set. Do not expect them to be like raspberry jam. I drop half a teaspoon of jam on a cold plate and drag my finger through to see if it leaves a channel, albeit a soft one. If not, add more lemon juice – another 2–3 tablespoons – and boil for a further 5 minutes. Do not cook for longer than 30 minutes or you will burn the sugar and the jam will have a caramel taste and syrupy texture.

Remove the jam from the stove and allow to cool for 10 minutes. Skim off any scum that has settled on the top and bottle the jam in hot, dry, sterilised jars. Cover with a clean towel and seal when cold. Label.

The French Pantry

Cherries come either sweet or sour. Sweet are for eating, sour are for cooking. Cooked sweet cherries lose some of their flavour, while the flavour of sour cherries will be enhanced once heated. As their name suggest they are a little tart, so need sugar.

Apricot Custard and Brioche Slice

Late in July, the first of the season's apricots began to appear – golden-orange orbs of preciousness. Jean-Claude at the Vic market, as well as having his *épicerie* stand, is also an orchardist and would arrive with trayloads of apricots that would be swarmed over by the locals, who would buy two and three trayloads at a time. Preserving is still a big part of the seasonal culinary chores in this area. Apricots turn their familiar orange colour before they have ripened, thus luring the unsuspecting buyer – and they will not ripen once picked. Jean-Claude dries the excess from the harvest for sale later in the year.

Prep time: 1 hour   Cooking time: 30 minutes   Serves: 8

1 x quantity Bread-maker Gâteau des Rois dough (see page 41)

Topping
1 cup milk
½ cup crème fraîche, cream or sour cream
2 tablespoons cornflour (if none to hand, use custard powder rather than flour)
2 tablespoons sugar
2 egg yolks (freeze the egg whites for use another time)
1 teaspoon vanilla paste, essence or extract
500 grams apricots, halved and stoned
icing sugar for dusting

Have the dough made and rested. Preheat the oven to fan bake 170°C (190°C standard) and place the rack just below the centre.

Heat the milk in a saucepan. Stir together the crème fraîche or cream, cornflour, sugar, egg yolks and vanilla to make a smooth paste. Whisk into the hot milk, and continue to whisk until the mixture thickens. Cover with a lid and set aside.

Roll the dough out to 1 cm thick and place on a shallow-edged tray, which can be any shape so long as the dough is only 1 cm thick. At this stage I leave the brioche dough for 10 minutes as, like all bread doughs, once rolled it shrinks a little. If required, use floured hands to push the dough back to the edges of the tray.

Spread the cooled custard on top, leaving an area of about 1 cm free of custard around the edge. Sit the apricots in the custard either cut side or rounded side up.

Bake in the preheated oven for 25–30 minutes until the dough is well cooked – it will be brown around the edges, but you need to make sure the centre is cooked, too. Sprinkle with icing sugar before serving. Serve warm with vanilla ice cream.

août

The vegetable tables at the markets were laden
with late-summer produce − red capsicums,
amethyst- and ivory-streaked aubergines,
courgettes, and tomatoes in every shape, size
and colour from golden yellow to scarlet red,
and their flavour was superb.

THE PACE OF LIFE MOVED UP A NOTCH when we turned the calendar over to August. We were frantic, trying to see and do as much as possible, be hosts-with-the-most for a revolving door of guests, and the action around us was clearly moving into top gear.

The *grand départ* (great depart) came and went. That's the weekend at the end of July where those who are on holiday depart homeward, and those going on holiday leave for their *vacances*, causing endless traffic jams; about 600 kilometres of queues were recorded by lunchtime. Other than in an emergency, this is not a day to drive. Not knowing this, I ventured out and when I spied the queues, I reversed just a tad too fast and put car, kids and all into a ditch! With so many people whizzing past, we had assistance in minutes to help *madame* and *les enfants* (the children), who were in some distress!

In our rustic village it looked, at least to the casual observer, as if the entire population of Paris had come south. The aged Renault 4L cars that rambled the back roads with their beret-topped and apron-clad occupants (think *'Allo 'Allo!*) were being overtaken by flash soft-top coupés, with Gucci sunglass-wearing, bronzed *messieurs* and astonishingly well-coiffured *mesdames*.

At holiday times, many city people return to their family's country home. With high rural unemployment, people have had to go to the city to find work. Under archaic inheritance laws, many old homes are empty apart from a month or two each year. Our area is full of farmhouses that have been left to tough out nature; sadly, many are losing the battle. For those seeking a quieter pace of life, or to raise children away from the commercialism of the modern world, there are many empty houses, needing just a bit of TLC, to encourage them here. That aside, the villages were buoyant and weekly markets crowded; restaurants required bookings; and laughter filled the air around the sidewalk cafés. It was the France of the tourist brochures.

The joviality was not just with the holidaymakers; farmers were now in harvest mode. The huge tractors that had become commonplace now looked like Mini Minors beside the lumbering harvesting machinery that rumbled along village laneways and into the fields. Our farmer neighbour invited Jean-Luc to join him high up in his harvester one evening. Jean-Luc's smile went from ear to ear as he was allowed to steer this behemoth!

Still needing more time in the sun were the fields of tobacco plants, which were gradually being deheaded of their pretty fairy-floss pink and white flowers, to ensure more nicotine in the leaf. Happy-faced sunflowers were beginning to dry, and burnished fields of wheat and barley were being baled for winter feed.

The forest-green fields of maize – they almost cover the southwestern area of France – had, with their towering height, turned country *chemins* (laneways) into tunnels. The rutted tracks left by tractors going through the maize made ideal cross-country paths for Jean-Luc and Olive-Rose to bike, run or play in. The maize would not be harvested for another two or three months. At night, these country *chemins*, lit only by the moon, became exceedingly hazardous. The ditches that flanked the roads were lost in summer undergrowth; watering systems, like giant lawn sprayers, unseen in the dark, would dump a torrent of water on the car, blinding vision. The eeriness was a bit like a scene from Harry Potter . . . awaiting the Death Eaters!

Assumption Day, 15 August, is a public holiday in France and also the day our village celebrates its heritage. Father Thierry-Joseph conducted a service of thanksgiving. Jean-Luc was serving, although I wasn't sure that his boardshorts and yellow Aussie T-shirt were quite suited to the role. Caixon's *église* (church) nestles on the southern side of the village, under towering plane trees and behind a crumbling old riverstone fence that is speckled with moss dehydrated in the summer heat. The worn stone steps tell of a once well-attended village church and every time I visit I wonder, if the walls could talk, what tales would they tell of this community. Built in the Middle Ages – probably of oak, elm or birch – its charcoal-grey stone walls enclose three majestic Baroque altars, hand-crafted in wood in the early eighteenth century and embellished with gilt by the finest carvers of the day, Marc Ferrère and family. Thus, hiding from time and tourists, in our village is a jewel of the Hautes-Pyrénées, loved but ageing.

Early in the mornings – the afternoon sun at 30-plus degrees was far too hot for anything other than a siesta – I cooked with the children, not always their favourites, but preserves. The stonefruit season continued as we welcomed plums; so beautiful to look at and eat. A few Quetsch, Agen, Mirabelle or Reine Claudes (greengages) placed together in a cracked or crazed Quimper faïence bowl on a weather-worn windowsill, created a still-life worthy of Van Gogh's brush.

Together we halved and stoned, simmered and stirred, making a pantry full of jam and a freezer full of poached fruit for pies and tarts in preparation for when winter called for hearty family puddings. We picked windfall apples, pears and wild blackberries, which grew wild through the laurel hedge on our property's border, for jelly. We did not get many blackberries, as neither the kids nor I could suffer the attacks of the triffid-like thorn-covered brambles; enough, though, to fill our memory banks with a fun morning.

Figs, the 'fruit of prosperity', finally arrived at the end of the month, some six weeks later than expected. The village laneways were awash with squashed figs and the birds were in fig heaven! I simply had to indulge in Anne Willan's caramelised fig Basque tart. Neighbours Peter and Lesley, who have far too many fig trees even for one village, said that a Basque tart had never tasted so good, but if you have it with crème anglaise, as Peter likes it, then it's five-star material!

Pomegranates made a brief appearance, their ruby jewel-like seeds adding colour,

PAGE 214, CLOCKWISE FROM TOP: *The Haute-Pyrénées to which we looked every day; flowering tobacco plants; a village shop in Saint-Bertrand-de-Comminges.*

THIS PAGE, CLOCKWISE FROM TOP LEFT: *Sunflowers in full bloom; Jean-Luc harvests the winter wheat behind Au Palouque; the village of Oloron-Sainte-Marie; Jean-Luc assisting Father Thierry-Joseph at the Assumption Day service at Caixon's église, St Martin.*

The course landaise events were memorable for participants and the crowd alike.

taste and texture to couscous salads. Charentais melons kept on coming week after week and at high season we could buy large, juicy, highly perfumed melons for one euro; melon for breakfast, lunch, dinner and afters. Coming from a city where these delicious fruits are expensive, even when in season, diving into half a melon after school was afternoon-tea heaven for my two.

The vegetable tables at the markets were laden with late-summer produce – red capsicums, amethyst- and ivory-streaked aubergines, courgettes, and tomatoes in every shape, size and colour from golden yellow to scarlet red, and their flavour was superb. We ate them like apples, or I baked them with lashings of olive oil, bulbs of fresh rose garlic, herbs from the garden – oregano, basil, parsley, chives or thyme – or ate them plain on Pascal's fresh baguette. Garlanded with salad leaves and crispy fried salami or *jambon*, they made a perfect one-dish salad meal. Fennel also became available in large or small bulbs, with or without their aromatic fluffy fronds. Ali would pick avocados, one to eat today, one for tomorrow and one to ripen later, so we could enjoy them at their peak. Different salad greens appeared weekly. We bought crunchy rose-red globe radishes, or pinky-finger-size pink and white ones, which only needed flaky salt from Béarn as accompaniment.

There were beans, not *haricots verts* (green beans), but fresh borlotti and Coco de Paimpol beans, which the locals here buy in boxloads for cooking into stews or soups, or simply to be preserved, either bottled or frozen. I set the children outside to pod them in the summer-scented courtyard, before simmering them with a bouquet garni – they only took 10 or so minutes to cook. Tossed in mustardy vinaigrette with herbs, diced tomato and handfuls of soft flat-leafed parsley, they made a hearty salad that could be further enhanced with sliced smoked duck breast or any of the salted meats of the area.

Coco beans don't look particularly attractive in their skins, but unwrapped they are white, buttery and delicious. Originating from Latin America, Coco de Paimpol has been grown since the late 1920s, when a French soldier brought seeds back to Brittany. After the Second World War, when there were major food shortages, coco beans proved a lifesaver for many people. They were granted AOC status (see page 224) in the late 1990s. The coco bean is used in hearty winter stews and casseroles like cassoulet, to accompany meat, or they can be eaten on their own, cooked with a ham bone, herbs and garlic – or whatever you fancy.

There was a plethora of activities for the kids, the problem being which to choose. Lessons at Poney Julie continued, the kids quite confident and loving the treks with Julie or Vanessa through the countryside, astride their favourite mounts.

A day at Trencalli, a *ferme pédagogique* (educational farm) nearby in Madiran, gave Olive-Rose and Jean-Luc hands-on experience at milking prize Jersey cows and making cheese and butter. Clad in gumboots and beret, Stéphane Vitse, who came south from Paris to find peace, runs one of a number of educational farms in the Hautes-Pyrénées where people of all ages, mainly children, can experience the day-to-day activities of farm life. Trencalli is mainly dairy, but we could also choose from farms where kids can mill wheat and make bread, or pick fruit and make preserves. We decided to stay the night with Stéphane, cuddling up in one of his *gîtes* (log cabins), so we could watch the wild deer roam through the oak and chestnut woods. It was a truly memorable night, under a star-studded sky unblemished by light pollution.

At wildlife parks we got up close and personal with animals such as Pyrenean brown bears, beavers and hawks that we usually only see on a National Geographic DVD. We trekked the mountains taking in the Cirque de Gavarnie, a Grand Site and a UNESCO World Heritage site, to watch *Beauty and the Beast* in cool mountain air in the natural amphitheatre that lies hidden between the mountain peaks. The two-kilometre walk in was picturesque and relatively easy, but the return journey was a bit of a nightmare, as we hadn't taken a torch with us and at midnight, that high up, midnight black means you cannot see anything; thank goodness for the torch app on a friend's phone!

From spring, but more so in summer when it's fête time, the *course landaise*, running of the bulls, and bullfights get underway. These events, which divide opinion, are associated more with Spain but are very popular in southwest France. Magnificently caparisoned horses and uniformed matadors, toreadors and rejoneadors are greeted by adoring fans, much as we'd hail the All Blacks. Signing sessions are de rigueur at the primary bullfights, as are pop-up souvenir shops selling posters, T-shirts, mugs and hats; it's like a pop concert.

While the bullfighting is not my thing, the *course landaise* events were a great spectacle, and we took in a number of these at nearby villages, mainly in the Gers, the region adjacent to the Hautes-Pyrénées. Fit, athletic young bucks in ornate velvet jackets, embroidered in silver or gold thread, pristine white shirts and trousers and colourful matching ties and cummerbunds, show their courage, daring and talent. The crowd hushes as the young men stand ready to challenge the animal, then twist and pirouette in the nick of time to miss a head-on collision. The Bandas – brass band – strike up foot-tapping tunes and the crowd roars. Judges signal the next challenge for the young torero and away it goes again. The kids loved it and so did we.

Sitting as a family beside enthusiastic locals, in a typical red and white open-topped village bullring festooned with banners and geraniums, enjoying an event that we will only ever see here, was the stuff of which memories are made, and I wished that summer would go on forever.

However, in the last days of August I woke one morning and flung the doors open to be met by a different air, clear and fresh, with a bite that lingered until later in the morning when the sun made an appearance. Summer, with its memories, was going, school was soon to start, and autumn had arrived literally overnight.

CLOCKWISE FROM TOP LEFT: *Ali, our fruiterer at the Vic-en-Bigorre market; flowers flourishing in a summer courtyard; Bigorre Valley; the village of Tillac; the Musée Massey at Jardtn Massey, Tarbes; summer greetings at the market.*

French and European Food Labels

Food labelling in Europe is a business in itself. Once only France had the long-standing and familiar *Appellation d'Origine Contrôlée* (AOC) label, but those times have passed. A plethora of European labels has been created to identify authenticity, origin, unique production and quality. The consumer who has shopped at the local village *marché* all her life would no more know or care about an AOP, IGP or STG, preferring to take the word of the familiar local retailer. Like it or not, though, change is on its way and some of the European labels sit alongside the purely French ones.

- *Label Rouge* (Red Label) is a French sign of distinction that guarantees a product is of a superior quality.
- *Appellation d'Origine Contrôlée* (Controlled Designation of Origin – AOC) classifies a product whose authenticity, originality and manner of production comes from its geographical origin. We know this label best from its use on French wine labels, but it has also been used on foods such as cheese, poultry, vegetables and more. However, this label is being replaced with the European AOP label, although not on French wine just yet.
- *Appellation d'Origine Protégée* (Protected Designation of Origin – AOP) will cover all dairy and food products (except wine) and is used to define a product's authenticity, originality and manner of production, which comes from its geographical origin.
- *Indication Géographique Protégée* (Protected Geographic Indication – IGP) extends the AOP identification system of products by their geographical origin, but includes products that may not be entirely manufactured/produced in the geographical origin area, although they still have quality, goodwill or other characteristics attributable to their geographical origin.
- *Spécialité Traditonnelle Garantie* (Traditional Speciality Guaranteed – STG) is a European label that does not take into account a product's origin, but rather its traditional composition manufacturing process.
- *Agriculture Biologique* (Organic Farming – AB) aims to encourage the conservation of soils, natural resources and the environment, and the preservation of local farming. Cultivation and breeding methods must exclude the use of chemical products and respect natural balances and animal welfare. Products must contain more than 95 per cent organic components.

Baking Basics

The arrival of French and Italian flours on New Zealand shelves certainly offers us choice, but also creates confusion as to what to use when. Imported sugars, mainly British but also French, along with European butters, create the same dilemma. Here's a brief guide in case you are inspired by French recipes from books or websites or you venture to buy imported French products now available in gourmet food stores.

Le Beurre – Butter

I miss French butter, the range of which was heaven for a confessed butteroholic. The main difference in flavour comes from the cream, which is cultured before churning to give French butter more complexity and sweetness. It may contain a slightly higher percentage of fat than ours, may be made from raw cream, and is available with varying degrees of salt content, which the French housewife will choose carefully according to the end use. Here's a compact list of terms and types.

- *Beurre fermier* or *beurre cru*, prepared by the farmer from raw cream, is highly perishable and sold at the farm gate or market. *Beurre laitier* is the same, but made in dairies.
- *Beurre pasteurisé* is butter made from pasteurised cream.
- *Demi-sel* or half-salted butter has 3–5 per cent salt.
- *Beurre fleur de sel* or *sel de mer* is an outstanding variation containing salt crystals that crunch between the teeth and tingle on the tongue.
- *Beurre salé* is salted butter containing 3–10 per cent salt.
- *Beurre fin* is churned butter that, by law, may be made with up to 30 per cent frozen cream.
- *Beurre de Baratte* (a favourite of mine) is a slowly churned butter.
- In addition, France has two AOC labelled butters, Beurre Charentes-Poitou from Aquitaine and Beurre d'Isigny from coastal Normandy.

La Farine – Flour

French flour was often a topic of conversation among British residents in France, as its grading is so different and the choice is so wide. The French grade their flour by ash content; that is, the residual mineral content left once an amount of flour is burned. In layman's terms, it will tell you how 'white' the flour is. Numbers range from 45, very white, to 150, which is as about as 'whole' as you can get. On the other hand, New Zealand flour is graded by protein content. Not all French flour types have exact substitutes in New Zealand. The information listed in the nutrition panel on the back of the packet is key if using French recipes for, say, bread or pastries.

French bread (white styles) is made with flour, of which the protein content should be no greater than 12–12.5 per cent – see the back panel of the product. Note: *farine de blé* translates to wheat flour.

- *Farine de Blé Type 150:* dark, wholewheat flour with added bran. Use stone-ground wholewheat as a substitute, or wholemeal with added bran.
- *Farine de Blé Type 110:* wholewheat/wholemeal flour.
- *Farine de Blé Type 80:* also called/sold as *semi-complète* or *farine bise*, it is fine in texture, beige in colour, with a light wholemeal-like flour flavour. It makes wonderful bread.
- *Farine de Blé Type 65:* a touch browner than white flour.
- *Farine de Blé Type 55:* called a soft wheat flour, with 11 per cent protein it is pretty much like our high grade flour, which has 12 per cent protein; use for bread, puff pastry and rich fruitcakes.
- *Farine de Blé Type 45:* a smooth, fine-milled flour with no endosperm, ideal to use in liquid preparations such as batters and pastries. Its protein is 9 per cent and our standard flour has 10.5 per cent, so it's not an exact substitute but as close as we can get.

Le Sucre – Sugar

The styles of *sucre* were as confusing as the flour; with marketing complexities and French descriptions, it was a sticky mess!

- *Sucre cristallisé* or *sucre cristal* is plain white granulated sugar.
- *Sucre en poudre* and *sucre en poudre extra fin* are equivalent to caster sugar.
- *Sucre glace* is icing sugar.
- *Sucre pour confiture* contains pectin for jam making.
- *Sucre vergeoise* prepared from beet sugar is moist brown sugar available *blonde* (light brown) and *brune* (very dark brown). The closest comparison I could make was muscovado and molasses respectively.
- *Cassonade* or *sucre roux de cassonade* is prepared from sugar cane; use raw sugar. Moist *cassonade* was similar to our soft brown sugar. It is available *cuivrée* (light coloured) or *ambrée* (dark); the best substitute would be moist brown sugar for the former and muscovado or a blend of the two for the latter.
- *Sucre en grains* or pearl sugar is large grains of sugar similar in size to broken rice; it will not melt when heated and is used for decoration.
- *Sucre vanillé* is vanilla sugar sold in 8-gram packets.
- *Sucre en morceaux* is sugar cubes.

Les Prunes

Summer's bountiful collection of stonefruit continued with the arrival of plums and prunes. They filled Ali's stand from summer to late autumn in a miscellany of shapes, sizes and colours.

Plums are royalty here, seated alongside Armagnac and foie gras at the VIP Gascon gastronomic table. Perfectly fresh at the point of sale, it was easy to see why they are so appreciated. No furry flesh, no bruised skins, just blushingly perfect fruits, sitting snugly together, dusted with a white coating that rubs off.

Reine Claude, with its vivacious green skin, is the first to market. A vintage variety, it is named after Claude, Duchess of Brittany, consort to Francis I of France in the 1500s, whose popularity has never waned. The Reine Claude was planted in England by Sir William Gage in the sixteenth century and became known as the greengage. If not eaten fresh, they are preserved as *confiture* (jam or conserves); their bright green dulls somewhat, but their flavour condenses; when spread on warm crusty bread, blissful!

The waxy, yellow-skinned little Mirabelle soon follows. About the size of a walnut, the Mirabelle is intensely sweet. Commercially, the juice is fermented into wine or distilled into highly alcoholic plum brandy, but I liked these tiny plums stewed and served with *crème anglaise* (custard) in some form.

Various blush-red-skinned, yellow-fleshed plums for eating only are crammed between the more famous named varieties all season. In August, the Quetsch – damson – arrives by the trayload. The juice is distilled to make the well-known *eau de vie* (brandy). Its deep crimson to heraldic purple skin conceals a rich yellow flesh that can be quite tart. When halved and sweetened with vanilla sugar, Quetsch are best baked into tarts.

My own favourite was the most famous of them all, the *prune d'Ente*, which is the finest for drying. Grown and dried in a designated area in the southwest, they can bear the label Pruneaux d'Agen AOC. To be able to buy new-season *moëlleux* (soft) prunes was a treat – the drying process stops at 35 per cent moisture, creating a soft, sweet, meaty prune with an intense plum flavour. Most prunes are dehydrated to about 23 per cent, caramelising the sugars, altering the flavour and giving a darker flesh but also making the prunes very hard. Water is added to rehydrate them before they are sold. The soft *moëlleux* prunes rarely lasted in our home, we all devoured them; I often added them to casseroles, where their sweetness unified and mellowed strong Gascony flavours such as duck and Madiran wine.

Mussels with Chorizo

Mussel season began in mid-July and we could not have missed their arrival. Signs decorated the motorway verges, counting down the days to the arrival of these much-adored, shiny blue-black shelled bivalves at the local supermarket. On their first appearance at Vic-en-Bigorre, the queue to buy them met us outside the *marché* entrance! France's beloved *moules frites* – mussels and chips – are apparently the second most popular dish in France behind duck, and featured repeatedly on café and restaurant menus in our area until late in the year. They were served steaming in well-worn authentic mussel pots: *à la soubise* (with onion sauce), *à la marinière* (in white wine) or *au safran et persil* (saffron and parsley) were a few styles that we enjoyed.

Prep time: 15 minutes   Cooking time: 15 minutes   Serves: 4

1–1.5 kilograms mussels
2 large shallots, peeled and diced (you can use half an onion, but shallots are sweeter)
3 cloves garlic, peeled and finely sliced (add more cloves if wished)
100–150 grams spicy chorizo sausage, finely diced
¾ cup white wine
¾ cup water
4 large tomatoes, blanched and peeled (choose only summer's best)
a good handful of finely chopped parsley

Pick over the mussels to make sure there are none with open shells. Put the open ones in a sieve and run under cold water; if they fail to close, discard. Clean the mussels as best you can.

Cook the shallots or onion and garlic until soft in a decent amount of olive oil in a large, lidded saucepan or deep-sided frying-pan (its shape is unimportant), big enough to effortlessly hold the mussels and with a tight-fitting lid to encase the steam. Add the chorizo and continue to cook until the deep ochre-red paprika-spiced fat runs from the sausage.

Working quickly, increase the heat, add the wine, water and tomatoes and bring to a rapid boil. Once boiling rapidly, add the mussels, cover and cook over a high heat for about 5 minutes – only until the shells open. Discard any whose shells have not opened. Add the chopped parsley, season with pepper and serve.

Pork and Pistachio Terrine

Having a terrine in the refrigerator over summer was a prerequisite for relaxed eating. A slice or two, a wedge of cheese and a baguette constituted a picnic by the Pont du Lys, the single-arched, hand-carved stone bridge over the river Lys at the bottom of our village. Here an old wooden picnic table tells the tale of village romances and broken hearts over many years through carved or chiselled names and initials inside hearts – and the odd one where the letter L for love had been turned into an H or crossed out altogether! We always tried to work out whose initials belonged to whom in our village and I could not help but think that the need for young lovers to announce their new-found romance like this was the same the world over.

Prep time: 30 minutes   Cooking time: 1¼ hours   Serves: 10–12

200 grams pork liver (or use chicken, lamb or beef liver)
milk, enough to cover pork
250–300 grams boneless rabbit or chicken
⅓ cup Armagnac or brandy
200 grams finely sliced bacon rashers
1 kilogram coarsely minced pork (not trim or lean pork, fat is required here)
6 shallots, peeled and chopped
1 egg
¼–⅓ cup shelled pistachio nuts (unsalted)
2 tablespoons flaky salt or 1 tablespoon finely milled salt
2 teaspoons coarsely ground black or white pepper
2–3 bay leaves (either fresh or dried; both are good to use in culinary terms)

Soak the pork liver in enough milk to cover while gathering the ingredients together. Do this to any liver if you wish to soften the strong liver flavour.

Cut the rabbit or chicken into bite-size chunky pieces and place in the Armagnac or brandy with a seasoning of salt and pepper. If you have the whole rabbit, add the kidneys as well. Cut the rind from the bacon and use the back of a knife – any knife will do so long as it is not sharp – to stretch the bacon rashers as thinly as possible, without tearing them. It's easier to do this if the bacon is not cold from the refrigerator – if it is cold it will tear.

Preheat the oven to 220°C.

Remove the pork liver from the milk and chop or mince finely. Place in a bowl with the rabbit or chicken and Armagnac or brandy, minced pork, shallots, egg, pistachio nuts, salt and pepper and mix well. Line the base and sides of a terrine dish – the shape does not matter but it needs to hold about 1.25 litres – with the bacon rashers, leaving the excess to hang over the edges.

Pile in the meat mixture and pack it in very firmly. Cover with the overhanging bacon rashers, weaving in the bay leaves at the same time.

Sit the terrine in a bain-marie and transfer to the preheated oven. Cook for 5 minutes, then lower the temperature to 170°C for 1 hour or until firm to the touch, or there are no pink juices when a skewer is inserted and withdrawn.

Carefully remove the terrine from the oven and bain-marie. Cover with foil and place a weight on top. Once cool, remove the weight and refrigerate. The flavours will be greatly improved if you can leave the terrine for a couple of days before eating. Keep covered in the refrigerator. If this mixture is divided into two terrines, the cooking time will be about 15 minutes less.

Baked Tomato Salad

Tomatoes at the *marché* came in a kaleidoscope of colours and shapes. Good old round tomatoes were always available, no variety given. Organic-looking heirloom varieties were sold labelled as *tomates anciennes*; sun-ripened, the best were to be found at AB (organic) stalls. For meatiness, the deeply creviced and peaked *coeur de boeuf* was hard to beat. Long-shaped tomatoes included the sublime pointed Andine Cornue, for which the only required adornment was vinaigrette and fresh herbs, and the simply luscious Torino. Long and rounded, when slow-roasted to perfection these oozed concentrated flavour over the palate. There were flavoursome plum tomatoes – great all-rounders for cooking and eating raw. *Tomates cerises* (cherry tomatoes), small red orbs of sweetness, dimmed a little beside the brightness of yellow or red *coeur du pigeon* (pigeon heart), which my children gobbled in preference to any other snack. Summer here was tomato heaven and we made this salad weekly – it's really a glorified baked tomato dish, which proved a favourite with our many guests.

Prep time: 10 minutes   Cooking time: 1–1½ hours   Serves: 6–8

12 tomatoes (choose only summer's best), halved
6 fat juicy cloves garlic, crushed but not peeled
1 teaspoon finely milled salt (more if using flaky salt)
1 teaspoon cracked pepper (I prefer the strength of white but black is fine)
1 teaspoon sugar
½ cup olive oil (choose one with a good flavour)
1 tablespoon each fresh thyme and oregano leaves

To finish
a loaf of crusty bread
8–10 slices *jambon*, prosciutto, pancetta or bacon

Preheat the oven to 160°C.

Place tomatoes in an ovenproof dish that will hold them all snugly. Scatter the garlic on top and season with salt, pepper and sugar. Drizzle the oil over the tomatoes. Scatter the herbs over.

Bake in the preheated oven for 1–1½ hours or until the tomatoes are cooked; the skins will have relinquished their firmness, but will still be able to hold their precious cargo, now softened and melting on the inside. Cool.

Cut half a dozen slices off the loaf of bread and tear into crouton-size pieces. Cook the *jambon*, prosciutto, pancetta or bacon in a little oil in a frying-pan until somewhat crispy. Set aside. Add the croutons to the pan and cook in the residue oil. Scatter the croutons and *jambon* or alternatives on top and adorn with fresh herbs of your choice.

Marie-Paule's Pine Nut Tuile

When Jean-Luc and I went to introduce ourselves to Marie-Paule, she cooked her Pine Nut Tuile. Unlike the small individual ones we normally see, Marie-Paule makes her tuile in a tray. When it is cooked and before it cools too much, she carefully rolls it over to resemble – as the name suggests – a tile the same size as tiles on the farmhouses of this area. Measurements are as given to me by Marie-Paule.

Prep time: 20 minutes   Cooking time: 25 minutes   Serves: 8

2 egg whites
pinch of salt
100 grams caster sugar
1 packet vanilla sugar (see The French Pantry below)
50 grams butter, melted
50 grams flour, sifted
125 grams pine nuts or pistachios
1 tablespoon rum

Preheat the oven to 150°C. Grease a 27 cm x 33 cm (approximately) baking tray, line with baking paper and grease again.

In a clean bowl, beat the egg whites, salt, sugar and vanilla sugar together until well mixed and thick. Add the butter. Stir in the flour, pine nuts or pistachios and rum. Pour the mixture into the prepared tray and spread out as evenly as you can.

Bake in the preheated oven for 20–25 minutes, or until the edges are well browned and the centre is firm. Remove from the oven, and while the tuile is warm carefully bring the longer edges together to resemble a semi-circular tile. If you have a large bottle, drape the tuile over it to help in this task. Once firm, transfer to a wire rack to cool. Break into pieces to eat.

The French Pantry

Vanilla sugar is commonly used in Europe, where it is readily available, to flavour sweet baked goods. It can easily be substituted with material from your cupboard; use 1 teaspoon sugar, either soft brown or caster, and 1 teaspoon vanilla essence or extract. The normal amount in a packet of vanilla sugar is 1½ teaspoons.

Summer Peach Frangipane Tart

The peach season, once it arrives, continues for months. With consistently long springs and summers and very cold winters, peaches and their stonefruit cousins grow well here. We ate them mostly fresh; a lunch or dinner here was never complete without a piece of fruit, although I have a penchant for poached peaches or peach and almond paired desserts.

Prep time: 20 minutes   Cooking time: 45 minutes   Serves: 8

300 grams shortcrust pastry

Filling
125 grams butter, softened
½ cup caster sugar
1 teaspoon almond essence
½ teaspoon vanilla essence (not essential but it will soften the almond essence)
2 eggs at room temperature, beaten
1 cup ground almonds
2 tablespoons flour, sifted
¼ teaspoon baking powder, sifted together with the flour
6 poached peaches, halved and stoned (see page 240; or for a shortcut use good-quality canned peaches)
¼ cup flaked almonds

Preheat the oven to 190°C. Place the oven rack just below the centre.

On a lightly floured board, roll the pastry out to a 26 cm diameter and place evenly over a 23 cm loose-bottomed flan or tart tin. Leave excess pastry hanging over the edges.

Beat the butter, sugar and essences together until light and creamy-looking – a wooden spoon, bowl and elbow grease will be fine for this task. Add the beaten egg a little bit at a time until it is well incorporated. (Cold eggs will cause the whipped butter and sugar to split, which will reduce the lightness of the finished frangipane.) Stir in the ground almonds and the sifted flour and baking powder. Spread over the flan and sit the peaches on top. Sprinkle the flaked almonds over.

Bake in the preheated oven for 40–45 minutes or until the filling is cooked.

Pain d'Épice Spiced Peaches

Peaches sat in row upon row at the summer markets . . . blushed orbs in hues from rose-tinted whitewash and peach pinks to saffron-washed orange. The peach season was marvellous; each luscious bite sent a fountain of juices running down the chin. To be able to buy peaches at that magical moment of ripeness was a cook's dream. Their perfume when inhaled deeply was redolent of an overwhelmingly sweet summer in bloom; we indulged daily.

Poaching summer stonefruit is no hard task. Prepare a poaching syrup of half sugar, half water or wine. You may need to adjust the sugar level if using a sweet wine, but ideally the poaching syrup should not be too sweet. Add flavourings – subtle ones like vanilla.

Prep time: 15 minutes   Cooking time: 15 minutes or 1 hour   Serves: 8–10

2 cups sugar
2 cups not-too-sweet white wine
1 cup water
1 vanilla pod, split, or 1 teaspoon vanilla essence or extract
¼–½ teaspoon Pain d'Épice spice mix (see page 36) or ground ginger
1–1½ kilograms peaches (use any variety so long as they are ripe)

Preheat the oven to 160°C.

Over a gentle heat, stir the sugar, wine, water, vanilla and spices together until the sugar has dissolved.

Halve the peaches and place cut-side up in a roasting dish. Pour over the syrup – there should be enough to come just to the top of the fruit. Cover with foil or a lid.

Bake in the preheated oven or, if you have a simmer mat, place on the lowest heat on the stove and cook gently until the peaches have softened. Never boil, as they will turn to pulp. The time will vary according to style of cooking and the ripeness of the fruit; the oven takes longer, about 1 hour, while fruit on top of the stove, being cooked by direct heat, will take about 15 minutes. The peaches should be firm enough to hold their shape but fairly soft when pierced with a skewer.

Turn off the heat and leave the peaches to finish cooking and cooling in the syrup. If the syrup is too thin for your liking, tip some off into a saucepan and boil to reduce to whatever consistency you prefer; cool before pouring back over the fruit. Serve with ice cream or decadent double cream.

septembre

Each September, the locals of Salies-de-
Béarn celebrate their salt-sprinkled history
with an event-filled La Heste de la Saü
(Salt Festival). The fête was a heavenly feast
of fabulous food and fun.

THE EXCITEMENT FOR BOTH CHILDREN of returning for the new school year was refreshing. Both moved up to the top year in their respective schools. With a male teacher, Matthieu, who was creative and keen on sport, Jean-Luc could not wait to go to school each day, although the return to winter school lunches – lentils and *fromage blanc* – wasn't so appealing for either of my children.

For me, the deadline for this book became a scary reality as I checked out how much remained undone! After the trials of the first few months, then finding my feet and gaining confidence, I had become carried away with excitement and enthusiasm for meeting producers, seeking out stories, soaking up the history of the area. It all piled up and meant little had been transformed into narrative!

Colleague, friend and sub-editor extraordinaire Joan Gilchrist arrived for three weeks to help me make sense of the jigsaw of ideas in my head, the trayloads of notes, a gallery worth of pictures and a freezer full of ideas, but no pattern for putting the pieces together. I love subs; for one thing they are happy to be the person behind the writer, and they also have a great knack for cutting out the inessentials. 'Don't say it in ten words, Allyson, if three will do.' I was back at school and my English report card was taking a hammering! Thank heavens I did not have to present it to anyone for sign-off . . . well, I did, as it all had to go back to Joan for editing. However, her presence ensured lots of work was done and some structure established.

In between the writing and the English lessons, there was still much to see and do. September was the middle of autumn and, while the mornings had turned cool, the late afternoons from 4 p.m. onwards were near 30°C, with no wind and glorious, clear skies; a delightful time to enjoy the area. Often at night the heavens performed, alight with electrifying and impressive thunder and lightning storms, common in this area during spring and autumn. We would gather on the Juliet balcony and watch the night show in awe of nature. I'm not a great one for technology, but with apps that allow watching the sky live, finding out about planets and stars is a sure and highly recommended way to have a great night with your kids.

The settled weather ensured that Au Palouque's garden continued to flourish. It was still overflowing with tomatoes, chillis, scarlet runner beans, lettuces and courgettes, although the peas were a dismal failure. What I could not garner myself was available at the Vic market, our weekly cornerstone activity.

Vic-en-Bigorre does not rate a mention in many tour books: the only one I found said that this large village could be a smaller Tarbes (our nearest town), which had a brutal write-up: 'grey, unfathomable toadstool of a departmental capital. There's precious little to see or do here; upon careful consideration you might be inclined to agree that among the towns of Southern France, Tarbes is the one most sadly wanting in personality and character.' Ouch!

However, it is here in these small towns, away from the main tourist haunts, that the real France exists. By September, I had fallen in love with our tiny patch, the people of the Hautes-Pyrénées and the Saturday morning market with its colourful stallholders and loyal local customers – it was a living movie set of characters of the variety you see in nostalgic 1950s black and white postcards. In Place du Halle, rusted old bikes leaned unsecured against the Halle du Marché's metal rails, and battle-weary Renault 4Ls and Citroën 2CVs filled the carparks.

Here is a France that has refused to change to a faster pace of life, where appreciation of simple pleasures and honest values are lived, not reminisced over. Early every Saturday, the kids and I would go, not only to buy but also to experience the real France, because a village market is not only about provisions, it is about meeting up for gossip! It's the one day when you see your neighbours or friends and hear the news. There's no rush to buy and move on; first the formal greeting to the stallholder, because even though you may have bought your one steak or six eggs from the same person each week for decades, it is the formal *vous* not *tu* that you use. Once the goods have been purchased, it's time to *tu* not *vous* to all your friends and catch up on the news.

I would soak up the scene, a liquorice allsorts mix of trundlers rattling past with their beret-topped owners; or a laden, frayed basket swinging on the arm of a child or an elderly *grand-mère*, weighing down the owner, who would look like a walking Tower of Pisa. The paella man, tucked beside the live animal department, would fill one corner of our *marché* with heady notes of saffron and tomatoes as his huge paella pan simmered away, the aromas competing for space with the confit and sarladaise potato chef at the other end.

By 10 a.m. the hall would be full of laughter, chatter, squawking birds being sold for the pot, strenuous bartering and, on special days, a local band playing a cross between Banda and Occitan music. How could I not enjoy this scene? It was not like trendy farmers' markets sprouting colour-coordinated boutique stands; this was life as it has always been. In some ways, unflattering reports of this town and its big-city sister have helped it remain authentic and faithful to its heritage; long may it last for the folks here. On these days, I believe fate played a hand when she gave us this village and the wider area for our adventure.

The children became regulars at many stalls. If I ever lost them I could guarantee they would be with the animals – mostly chickens, ducks, pigeons, guinea fowl, quail, but also pet rabbits, kittens, etc. One week I asked Jean-Luc to buy a black French beret for a gift, but the beret seller was *en vacances* (on holiday) and, with loose change burning a hole in his pocket, Jean-Luc grabbed his chance to buy a pet, something we had assiduously avoided given the logistics of bringing an animal back to New Zealand.

Grinning from ear to ear, Jean-Luc bore his acquisition (bartered down from five to

PAGE 244, CLOCKWISE FROM TOP LEFT: *Local sign posts; bread seller at the Vic-en-Bigorre market; homeward bound from the markets; the village of Saint-Sever-du-Rustan.*

THIS PAGE, CLOCKWISE FROM TOP LEFT: *St. Martin's church in Vic-en-Bigorre; a Renault 4L, the local car of choice; the Vic-en-Bigorre town hall; a local's bike rests outside a bar in Maubourguet.*

two euros) up the street to our regular coffee spot, Café Bigourdan. Here he proudly placed on the bar his new, mottled-grey, fluffy, beady-eyed baby duckling! Greeted by squeals of laughter from the ladies, the duckling promptly pooped over the bar, circumnavigating the odd beer! Madame Toulouse rushed for a lidded box for safe duck transport and kindly cleaned up the mess, suggesting that Jean-Luc and Olive-Rose find their parents before creating any further mayhem!

Luck was on our son's side as we had a guest, thus preventing his father from losing his rag, as happens when pets are somewhat forced upon parents! From then on, each week Madame the duck seller would wink at the kids – and laugh heartily at their mother!

It is the beret more than any other item that we immediately associate with Frenchmen, and, while it is not so popular with younger city dwellers, it is still de rigueur wear in rural areas, especially in the south. Sadly, though, even the ubiquitous French beret has gone the way of mass production in Asia.

Turning this trend around and actively trying to save the locally made beret industry is enthusiastic Irishman Mark Saunders. He has taken on the management of Laulhère, one of the last remaining beret-manufacturing companies, based in the delightful town of Oloron-Sainte-Marie in the Béarn, the region next to ours. Mark willingly gave up his time to show me the A–Z of beret-making.

Using a traditional pattern, one kilometre of fine New Zealand or Australian merino wool thread is knitted into an oversized beret, before it is felted, dyed and finished with lining, band and leather rim. There are more than 20 steps in the manufacturing process, seven of which are quality checkpoints. In all, it takes eight hours to make a beret. With Paris-based ad agencies, an ambitious international PR plan and new twists on old designs, Mark looks well on the way to saving the beret.

Further on from Oloron-Sainte-Marie is the prettiest village of the region, Salies-de-Béarn. Here, each September, when it's cooler and all the whistle-stop tourists are back home sorting their photographs, the locals celebrate their salt-sprinkled history with an event-filled La Heste de la Saü (Fête du Sel or Salt Festival), and I was warmly welcomed to join a small media group for the weekend.

In mediaeval times, an abundance of salt springs, with between seven and 10 times more sodium chloride than found in sea water, ran through this area, leading to the establishment of a vibrant town; salt was all the residents produced. Their homes within the village walls had one room to live in, with the rest of the space given over to salt production, which requires heat to evaporate the water. Today that heat comes from sun and electricity, whereas in the past it was from open fires. The process involved the entire family working to make the salt. In time, 500 villagers established the Corporation of Salt Producers, setting down rules regarding salt production to ensure that Salies did not lose its industry to others. Some 500 years on, the Corporation still exists and its members, who must be direct descendants of the original families, still manage aspects of salt production today in Salies, including the fête.

For four days, the village is vibrant. Stalls and shops, which are set out on the cobblestoned laneways in a snail-shell spiral design radiating from the town square, seem to go on and on. At each turn, there are yet more local culinary treats to savour. Restaurants spilling onto the roads serve local specialities like Garbure, duck confit and the highly prized Jambon de Bayonne (cured and aged ham from the Bayonne region). This ham must be cured using only Salies de Béarn salt to earn its label of origin logo.

The celebratory Sunday Mass, conducted in Occitan, the old language of this area, is a pageant of French culinary history. Led by brass bands, dignitaries from many local producer associations – snail farmers, beekeepers, winemakers, cheesemakers and, of course, salt producers – all formally attired in plush velvet embroidered gowns, with elaborate hats and medals of office, parade through the main streets and into church for a service to celebrate tradition, culture and history. For a history-loving foodie, the fête was a heavenly feast of fabulous food and fun, including a lively parade of decorated floats through the town.

The final event, which everyone turns out to watch, is the Running of the Salt Pails. The girls and women dress in traditional peasant costumes. Working as a team of two, they must each carry 20 litres of water in traditional wooden vessels called *herrades* on their heads, along the village's main street, round corners and over a bridge to return not just first, but with the least amount of spillage.

The men, representing the *tiradous* or brine bucket porters, traditionally clad in belted, coarse sacking *tabards* over T-shirts with soft, loose leggings, blue neckerchiefs and black berets, run in pairs carrying 92-litre *sameaux* (wooden buckets) of water hung on sturdy poles. Their course featured a tight turn around a wine barrel which, accompanied by a measure of male bravado, ensured a spectacular finale to a wonderful fête. The winnings? The same for all: village honour. What else? This is France.

Before the month was out, the kids, Warwick and I joined a group of Caixon locals for a walk. Well, our interpretation of the poster was a 'walk'. We very soon learned that '*balade gourmande*' (gourmet walk) had nothing to do with food and, when linked to the words '*sentier de randonnée*' (hiking trail), became a 12-kilometre intensive off-road hike through sodden cornfields and up substantial chestnut-forested hills over rutted tracks, rather than the gentle ramble we expected. The discovery of a large section of Roman road, even today used as a boundary divider for properties, had Jean-Luc acting out Professor Mick Aston from *Time Team* with an Inspector Clouseau accent, creating much merriment. A four-course lunch with plenty of wine followed – a great pick-me-up – and late in the day four weary walkers wandered home with lots of memories. We may not speak much French, but we now had enough to join in and feel very much a part of things.

Each village here is known for an event; ours for historical walks and Sombrun, next door, for its Fête du Cheval. The weekend featured pony treks, gymkhana competitions, carriage races and show jumping. Between the MC perched in his custom-made media stand – a battered cart behind a tractor – giving a detailed commentary, and the non-

riding children participating in those comical races that seemingly enjoy world-wide popularity, such as sack races, wheelbarrow races, three-legged and egg and spoon races, the whole weekend reminded me of my childhood Sunday School picnics.

Two of France's national parks are in the southwest, and as we bordered the Parc National des Pyrénées we were afforded the most spectacular scenery to tramp in, parks and zoos to visit, while the unique wildlife of the area was a privilege to see.

We enjoyed an overnight stay in a trampers' cabin at the Parc Animalier des Pyrénées where we were up close and personal with wolves – albeit through a large glass wall – and able to watch at first hand the pack behaviour as they fought for food. In the mornings before the park opened one could help feed the playful beavers, majestic ibex, enchanting chamois and even the fearsome Pyrenean brown bear, soon to go into hibernation.

The bear, once extinct here, was reintroduced to the mountains in 1995, but as this area is home to several hundred thousand sheep in the summer months, farmers' fears have risen and now the bear's 'wild' future looks dim.

Next village over, at Beaucens, we caught a thrilling falconry display at the Donjon des Aigles – the Eagle Keep – in the grounds of an eleventh-century château, which has surrendered to ageing. The ruins have been imaginatively reinvented, to become a sanctuary for one of the world's finest collection of birds of prey – eagles, falcons, owls, vultures and one thoroughly intimidating condor.

All these birds performed to music (by The Eagles – I kid you not!) for over an hour, flying majestically through the grounds of the château and down into the valley below. The show finished with all the children feeding the finches, little parrots and budgerigars; what great memories.

In the last days of the month, Fabrice, our neighbour and winemaker at Château Montus, escorted me around his company's vineyards to see the grape harvest in progress. Friendly, hard-working Spaniards had travelled some 1000 kilometres from Andalusia for two weeks' hard work, leavened by witty commentary and local songs. Fabrice had his work cut out for him this year. The harvest was 4–6 weeks late after nature's unscheduled cold and very wet spring. Botrytis had appeared and there had been less sunshine to ripen the grapes, but in true pragmatic French fashion Fabrice shrugged and said '. . . *pfft*, you cannot change what you cannot change'.

Throughout the region harvesting continued. The sunflowers, standing like charred sticks, were finally being deheaded. Tarbais beans were being hand-picked, although some were left to dry on the vine. Tobacco leaves had been cut and hung from rafters to dry. The corn, now hues of wheaten-gold and fading moss green, still stood and would do so until the following month; it must be very dry before harvesting. In some areas, fields of green-stemmed corn had been harvested and chomped to mush in one swoop of a harvester to be used for cattle feed.

My harvest, too, by month's end was more or less complete. Sadly, I took the spade and rake to the garden that had given me so much pleasure throughout the year. I pulled up the plot's fences and trellis and turned the soil over, covering my chip-covered walkways and memories with sweet-smelling earth, putting it all back to the same condition in which I found it, as agreed with our property's owner.

Once colour- and produce-filled, the now fallow plot would be covered with the clippings of pruned fruit and laurel trees, a task for next month.

CLOCKWISE FROM TOP LEFT: *Jean-Luc with Donald the duck; la Fête du Mouton, Larreule; the men's salt race at Salies-de-Béarn; Monsieur Vignaux (centre) barbecues for us; the girls' salt race; modelling the beret of the area, which protects the wearer from the weather – be it snow, rain or sun.*

Fabrice Dubosc, Winemaker

Madiran, a pretty little village just 10 minutes from Caixon, sits at the northernmost tip of the Hautes-Pyrénées. It is also the name given to the AOC red wines of the area (the whites are known as Pacherenc du Vic-Bilh). The total designated growing area also takes in land in the adjacent departments of Gers and Pyrénées-Atlantiques.

Regrettably, Madiran wine is little known; it has been eclipsed by the likes of Champagne and Bordeaux. However, that's changing thanks to local visionary Alain Brumont and his talented team of winemakers, one of whom, Fabrice Dubosc, lives in our village and was the first person to *faire bon accueil* (welcome) us.

Our daughters were in the same class at Caixon Maternelle, and I am sure Fabrice saw the near panic on my face as I dropped Olive-Rose off to school in that first week. He is your quintessential man of southwest France with elegant manners, and is a charming conversationalist and passionate gourmet of the wine and the rich indulgent food of this area.

Up until two decades ago, Madiran wines were considered heavy, tannic, mediocre and unapproachable to drink, until the wines – especially the reds – spent several years sleeping off the tannin before hitting the shelves for sale. Even then, further keeping was warranted. This cast a long shadow on the wines' reputation, perhaps less than fairly. But now Alain Brumont is leading the way in re-inventing the image of Madiran.

Alain's two Châteaux, Montus and Bouscassé, produce 25 per cent of the total Madiran *appellation*, though it was not always thus. Thirty-five years ago, Alain, then a farmer, had an epiphany and upended his life to go winemaking. What followed has been a lifetime of dedication to the wines of the southwest, in particular to the much-criticised Tannat grape. With greater care given to the choice of *terroir*, viticulture and viniculture, and expanding his talent base with innovative winemakers, Alain has transformed the Tannat grape into one that now sits beside the noble greats like Pinot Noir or Shiraz.

For Fabrice, Alain's groundbreaking work was exciting and well known. A serendipitous meeting on the ski fields when Fabrice, also a trained ski instructor, helped Alain's son after a stumble, led to him joining Alain's team. Fabrice is a native of Gascony and an oenologist with an exceptional curriculum vitae. Thirteen years on, he is now Chief Winemaker and Alain's right-hand man, and has gained a reputation for adding elegance and finesse to the wines by using less oak on the whites, bottling them earlier and overseeing better handling of the reds during oak maturation.

The harvest that year had been *fou* (crazy), according to Fabrice. The seasons, which should run like clockwork, had not. Summer had gone, autumnal colours were

weaving their way through the vineyard, but still Fabrice was hanging out for a little more sun on the 250 hectares he oversees. The grapes were not yet sweet enough and the stems, which must turn to brown before picking, were an army-green hue . . . so he waited.

When the time was finally right, Fabrice invited me back to see the harvest action. I found him camped at the château for the month in order to be on site as the grapes arrived. During sunlight hours Spanish pickers were out in force hand-picking flawless bunches that would, in time, become the company's top echelon wines – Chateau Brumont, Montus and Bouscassé – which are exclusively sold through the cellar door and fine wine shops. Throughout the night, machine-picked fruit, destined for second-tier labels that sell in supermarkets, arrived and Fabrice directed production.

Fabrice has a keen eye on the wines of the New World. Pinot from the South Island of New Zealand, he says, is a favourite. He believes that the AOC regulations restrict innovation, holding back opportunities for winemakers to revitalise old or lesser-known areas and introduce grape varieties that may better suit the area – but this is France and change is hard to achieve. To circumnavigate the restrictions, young winemakers are moving away from producing AOC labelled wines, growing different grape varieties and producing exciting wines under innovative new labels.

However, Fabrice explained that it is a long-term and uphill marketing and public relations battle. Find a flash restaurant anywhere in the world and give the patron a choice between an AOC and a non-AOC bottle, and most will go with the former. It's like corks. He praises New Zealand for using screw tops, which he prefers since the wine does not go off, but when he asks people why they want corks, he says, he always gets the same reply – they like the sound of the pop. He retorts, '*pfft* . . . so they want music not wine; what can you do?'

The future looks good in Madiran. Fabrice, like many winemakers here, believes that the popularity of the notable wines of last century is declining and that people are looking for new names, lighter styles with more fruit. The New World wines, like New Zealand's, he says, are technically excellent and have helped bring new ideas, from production to manufacture and consumption trends. Cross-fertilisation of ideas is assisted by an annual influx of a united nations of young winemakers, who arrive to do harvest with Fabrice. So far there have been no Kiwis, but they would be exceptionally welcome.

Roast Spiced Chicken

At the market each week we were able to buy wonderful fresh *poulets fermiers* – chickens direct from the farmer. Their golden skin and sweet flesh is a result of a diet of locally grown maize. I would regularly see beret-wearing farmers driving through Caixon with a deep-sided trailer hitched to the back of their rusty, smoke-belching tractors, full to overflowing with maize, en route to home to fatten up the chickens, ducks or livestock. Often they would stop at the crossroads outside our *maison* (house) and chat to their mate coming the other way; no hurry, no pressure. I loved this scene, it was like watching a real-live 1950s movie. Serve this delicious spiced chicken with halved roasted onions and extra chestnuts, or with roasted red onions or shallots.

Prep time: 30 minutes   Cooking time: about 2 hours   Serves: 6–7

¼ cup milk
2 tablespoons Armagnac or brandy
100–150 grams Pain d'Épice, crumbed (see recipe page 35)
1 onion, peeled and finely diced (use a white onion if you have one)
2–3 cloves garlic, crushed, peeled and mashed to a paste with salt
100 grams butter
500 grams pork mince (it must be coarsely ground)
8–10 whole chestnuts, bottled or canned, chopped into pea-size pieces
1 egg
1 large chicken for roasting (remove any bits remaining inside)

Preheat the oven to 180°C.

Sprinkle the milk and Armagnac or brandy over the Pain d'Épice. Cook the onion and garlic in a knob of the butter until soft. Cool.

Mix together the Pain d'Épice, onion mixture, pork mince, chestnuts and egg. Season.

Stuff the chicken cavity with the pork mixture. Tie the legs together loosely and sit the chicken in a roasting dish. Spread the remaining butter on top of the chicken. Any leftover stuffing can be rolled into balls, wrapped in bacon rashers or *jambon* and added to the roasting dish in the last hour of cooking. Add halved onions and extra chestnuts too, if wished.

Roast in the preheated oven for around 2 hours or until the chicken is cooked.

Use any fat and juices remaining in the dish to make gravy, if wished.

Borlotti Bean Salad

Come summer, fresh shelling beans arrived at the market, albeit only for a short time. Shelling beans, as their name suggests, require shelling before eating, as opposed to green beans, which are eaten in their entirety. Shelling beans can be eaten early and, like sugar snaps, you can eat the pod as well; or later in the season when the bean has matured but is still fresh – this was my favourite – or at the very end of the season when the pods have withered and the bean on the inside is dry. The kids and I would sit on Au Palouque's steps late in the day when it was cool and pod crimson-streaked, pale greeny-lemon borlotti beans (and the more robust-looking Coco de Paimpol when we could get them) that revealed grey-white pearls mottled with pink on the inside. Sadly, the beans turned greyish-purple when cooked, but tossed with fresh summer salad foods, they made marvellous meals.

Prep time: 20 minutes   Cooking time: 15 minutes   Serves: 2–3

500 grams fresh shelling beans, in the pod
½ large red or white onion, peeled and finely diced
1 clove garlic, crushed, peeled and sliced
½ cup fine-tasting olive oil
1 long mild green chilli, sliced (deseed if wished)
¼–½ teaspoon ground *piment d'Espelette* (or paprika and a pinch of chilli)
4–6 slow-baked tomatoes (prepared as per recipe page 234)
1 cup well-packed salad and or soft herb leaves (the choice is yours)
1–2 teaspoons balsamic vinegar

Pod the beans and cook – like rice or pasta – in boiling salted water for 10–12 minutes until tender; drain well.

Gently cook the onion and garlic in the olive oil until crisp-tender; you do not want them raw, but likewise not too soft – a little bite is ideal. Toss in the chilli and *piment d'Espelette*, and once the sizzling stops toss through the beans.

When the beans are just warm, chop the tomatoes and fold through the beans with the salad or herb leaves of your choice. Finish with a drizzle of balsamic vinegar and serve. A slice or two of grilled *jambon* makes a tasty partner, but crispy cooked smoked bacon would be equally delicious.

Duck and Olive Paella

With so much duck confit crammed onto the pantry's shelves and summer still beaming down, I added the portions along with spicy chorizo-style duck sausages to my favourite paella recipe, in which I was also able to use my home-grown saffron.

Prep time: 45 minutes   Cooking time: 40–50 minutes   Serves: 8

½ teaspoon saffron threads
½ cup dry white wine
4 portions duck confit (see recipe page 90)
6–8 thin, spicy-flavoured duck (or pork or lamb) sausages
¼ cup olive oil
1 large onion, peeled and finely diced
1 green or red capsicum, chopped
4–6 large cloves garlic, crushed, peeled and sliced
3 cups short-grain or paella rice (the latter is nice but not essential)
2 teaspoons paprika, plain or smoked (both are fine)
1 teaspoon salt
1 bay leaf
1 cinnamon stick
3 large juicy tomatoes, diced (blanch and peel first, if you feel the need)
5½ cups chicken stock
1 cup green olives

Preheat the oven to 190°C.

Stir the saffron into the wine and set it to one side. Wipe as much fat as you can from the duck confit portions and place on a baking tray. Cook in the preheated oven for 15 minutes, while you prepare the rest of the paella.

Brown the sausages evenly – do not cook all the way through – and set aside.

Add the oil to a large, wide frying-pan or paella pan or a roasting dish that is flame-proof and ovenproof. Cook the onion, capsicum and garlic until softened.

Add the rice, paprika, salt, bay leaf and cinnamon stick and stir to coat in the oil and onion mixture before adding the saffron-infused wine, tomatoes and stock. Simmer for 5 minutes, stirring occasionally. Remove the duck from the oven, sit the portions in the rice with the olives and sausages and cover – I use foil.

Cook in the preheated oven for 15–20 minutes. Take a peep: the rice should just about be cooked and the cooking liquid almost evaporated. Remove from the oven, but do not lift the foil, and keep in a warm place for 5 minutes before serving.

Fig and Almond Tart

There was at least one fig tree in every *jardin* (garden) in the villages around us, and when the fig season finally arrived, it was short, sweet and full of competition from the birds. What this tart lacks in eye appeal it makes up for in taste.

Prep time: 15 minutes   Cooking time: 25 minutes   Serves: 6–8

half-quantity Allyson's Quick Flaky Pastry (recipe follows) or 300 grams puff pastry
75 grams butter, softened (unsalted is best)
¼ cup plus 2 tablespoons caster sugar
a dash of almond essence
¾ cup ground almonds
2 tablespoons fig jam
2 tablespoons flour
10–12 fresh figs

Preheat the oven to 190°C. Grease or line a baking tray with baking paper.

Roll out the pastry to a 30 cm x 25 cm oblong and place on the tray. The edges do not have to be perfect. Refrigerate while preparing the topping.

Beat the butter, sugar and almond essence together until light and fluffy. Stir in the ground almonds, jam and flour. Spread over the pastry, leaving a 2 cm border free of filling. Halve or quarter the figs and place cut-side up on top of the filling.

Bake in the preheated oven for 25 minutes or until golden and well-cooked.

Allyson's Quick Flaky Pastry

Prep time: 15 minutes   Makes: 700 grams

3 cups flour
½ teaspoon salt
275 grams butter, chilled and chopped roughly
1 egg, beaten with 6 tablespoons very cold water

Put the flour, salt and butter into a food processor and pulse until the mixture looks like large peas. Pulse in the egg and water. The mixture should be coarsely clumped together. Turn out and bring together on a floured bench.

Roll out to about a 30 cm x 15 cm oblong with the shorter edge parallel with the bottom of the bench. Fold the bottom third of the pastry over the centre third. Bring the remaining third down on top, so that you have three layers. Re-roll and repeat this process twice more. Wrap and refrigerate for 1 hour, or up to two days, before using.

Greengage Jam

Nothing beats the flavour of home-made jam, and Reines Claudes, as the French call greengages, are simply the best when made into jam, as their deep plum flavour intensifies. Often the children would help me; that was until the sun shone too much and their friends came calling on bikes or scooters and then they'd be gone. I'd find them later skimming stones at the Lys River at the bottom of the village.

Prep time: 20 minutes   Cooking time: 30 minutes   Makes: 7–8 x 300 gram jars

1.5 kilograms greengages
1 cup water
¼ cup lemon juice (do not use Meyer lemons; choose a thick-skinned lemon)
1.5 kilograms sugar

Wash the plums, de-stem if required, halve and stone. Put the cut fruit in a large preserving pan with the water and lemon juice and bring slowly to the boil, crushing the fruit with a wooden spoon.

Once the fruit has softened to a pulp, add the sugar and stir over a moderate heat until the sugar dissolves. Increase the heat and boil rapidly – as fast as you can, as the faster you can achieve a set, the finer the flavour of the jam will be. Long boiling diminishes the flavour.

Boil for 10 minutes, stirring occasionally. Remove from the heat and test for a set. To do this, place a spoonful on a cold saucer and run your finger through the middle; if the jam makes a channel, then it has cooked sufficiently. If this is not the case, return to the boil and try again in 5 minutes. Whatever you do, do not leave the jam boiling while you are testing it for a set, as it may overcook and become toffee-like.

Remove from the heat and bottle into hot, dry, sterilised jars. Cover with a clean tea towel and seal when cold. Don't forget to label and date.

Heavenly when served atop toasted and well-buttered brioche.

The French Pantry
If using *sucre pour confiture* (jam-setting sugar), which is ideal here, omit the lemon juice.

octobre

Next to duck, foie gras and red wine, you must, if you wish to be considered local, serve *cèpe*, *girolle* or *trompette de la mort* mushrooms, all of which are to be found in the woods surrounding Caixon.

NATURE'S STOPWATCH CLICKED OVER once I turned the calendar to October. The leaves on Au Palouque's cherry and oak trees fell like constant gentle rain, fluttering down in intermittent breezes, tapping on windows before rustling in whirls to the ground and being caught in *fossés* (ditches) or hiding in the corners of our old stone walls, creating a natural compost heap. Unlike our country's evergreens, France's mainly deciduous trees present a palette of autumnal shades; hues from champagne creams to burnt vermilion and dark brick reds so intense that they could only have been created by nature.

As we wandered home from school in the weeks preceding yet another stretch of school holidays, we collected leaves to make a poster about the shades of Caixon. It was a way that, together, we could discover nature, and I could pass on all those facts I learned so long ago at Girl Guides . . . over steaming hot Milo in cooling night air, with Mum recalling the 'old days' (only the 1970s!), kids laughing; special memories.

Although today's farmers are computer savvy and have high-tech machinery, around us the farmers were following their seasonal routine, seemingly little changed over the generations. Despite all the twenty-first-century technology, farming is still a 24-hour, seven-days-a-week job until winter sets in. But the actual farming is much changed. Fewer than 25 per cent of all French live in rural areas and an even smaller percentage on farms. Overall, the days of families living under one roof and farming have almost gone, although this area still has generations of families living in the same village, or at least nearby.

Economic forces and modern living have ensured change so that farming is less bucolic and more agri-business! Many farmers here are unable to live entirely off the land, despite the continuing existence of substantial subsidies. Thus, many farming households have a second income stream – a salaried working partner, or using their farmhouse to offer *gîte* holiday accommodation. Others have established *fermes pédagogiques*, educational or tourist facilities where schoolchildren and visitors pay a fee to spend a day gaining hands-on experience of various aspects of farming.

Mother Nature was still not playing ball. The old-timers in my village advised that this was due to this year having 13 moons – an old wives' tale, maybe with an ounce of truth? Whatever the reason, unseasonable rain made harvesting of the dried maize impossible and delayed the turning of the soil and the planting of winter wheat, creating much angst.

However, the dried Tarbais bean harvest was in full swing. The beans, which grow up the corn stalks, looked withered and mouldy but once split, nestled inside were naturally dried, perfect, shiny white beans, prized for their taste and texture – a staple of the diet here and the preferred bean for garbure and cassoulet.

Ducks, too, were heading towards harvest and market – autumn and winter is when ducks have the best flavour and, of course, the much venerated foie gras is produced. On the main road outside our village, Montfort, a large enterprise, produces an extensive array of duck-based products for local and export markets. Each day ducks arrived by the truckload, much to my kids' entertainment. 'So many Donalds,' remarked Olive-Rose. With one duck for every two Frenchmen – and there are over 60 million of them – the importance of *le canard* in French culture and cooking cannot be underestimated, especially here in southwest France where duck is the foundation ingredient of the local cuisine.

As a cook who likes her children to know about food and its origins, I rounded them up for a day on a duck farm. Philippe and Baptiste Carrère, a father and son team, farm some 25,000 ducks annually on their 45-hectare farm, Les Délices du Luy de France, in a nearby village. Their produce is sold both fresh and canned, the latter having won medals at France's prestigious Concours Générale Agricole. Each week 500 80-gram hatchlings arrive to be nurtured until culling at 15 weeks. Baptiste swooped in to the mêlée of week-old ducklings keeping warm under heat lamps in an insulated shed to gather a handful of noisy, fluffy balls for the kids to hold; as expected, they 'ooed' and 'aahed' on cue!

Later, reality struck when Baptiste demonstrated how they dissect, gut, remove the precious foie gras and then prepare the ducks for market. Both kids pulled faces that made me laugh, but they did not walk away, taking in Baptiste's lesson on duck farming from production to marketing with a tolerable interest. I'll make cooks of them yet!

On the odd day when the sun shone and there was a breeze, our village was permeated with the cigar-like aroma from the tobacco, which was picked last month and hung in barns and makeshift hothouses and was now almost dry. At the end of the month, local women will come and prepare the 60,000 stems in our neighbours' hothouses for despatch, removing the central veins and packing only the wafer-thin, leathery brown leaves.

October also heralded the much anticipated mushroom season. Next to duck, foie gras and red wine, you must, if you wish to be considered local, serve *cèpe*, *girolle* or *trompette de la mort* mushrooms, all of which are to be found in the woods surrounding Caixon. So popular is mushroom collecting that a new law lays down that you may only gather them within the boundaries of your village commune, and you must carry a certificate from the Mayor verifying that you are from the village. Should you stray beyond the village boundary, on your own head be it! Often here, when word of an exceptional harvest spreads, *gendarmes* arrive to patrol the laneways and act as a 'deterrent' to any disputes over boundary rights – only in France!

One chilly morning I joined Maurice Vignaux, our Mayor's husband, on a clandestine *cèpe*-finding mission. Meeting others as we walked into the forests, Maurice advised me to wait while other walkers moved off elsewhere – after all, this was a covert operation! Then

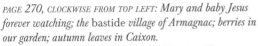

Ⓐ CÈPE DE BORDEAUX : DE 12 à 20 €/Kg
Ⓑ CÈPE D'ÉTÉ (RÉTICULÉ) : DE 12 à 20 €/Kg
Ⓒ TRÉMOULET (BOLET ORANGÉ) : 9,00 €/Kg
    BOLET PIED ROUGE : 1,50 €/BARQON
Ⓓ ... COMMUNE : 3,30 €/BARQON
        ... 90 € /BARQON

PAGE 270, CLOCKWISE FROM TOP LEFT: Mary and baby Jesus forever watching; the bastide *village of Armagnac; berries in our garden; autumn leaves in Caixon.*

THIS PAGE, CLOCKWISE FROM TOP LEFT: Monsieur Vignaux, cèpe hunter extraordinaire; me at a local duck farm; autumn's mushroom bounty; makeshift stall for selling foraged mushrooms at the local markets.

we stepped stealthily through the chestnut and oak forest, foraging in duvet-thick, leafy undergrowth for the mysterious *cèpes*. Each time we found some, Maurice would laugh deeply with a whoop of 'hey hey hey', light a cigarette and expound in a deep southwest accent '*Regardez*, Allyson, *regardez*!' At first, I was slightly perturbed at my uselessness to *regarder* and find, but in time I learned to spot these ingeniously camouflaged icons of the culinary fungi world. Back home, Madame Vignaux cooked fresh *cèpes* with garlic and parsley for me; the only, only way to eat them, I was told. I later made a *cèpes*-loaded pasta carbonara for all of us to share; with 5 kilograms for our morning's work, it was one sure way of using up so many.

Late in the month the Basque town of Espelette came to life with the Fête du Piment d'Espelette – a joyous, three-day celebration of the locally grown red chilli pepper, its harvest, history and cuisine, and of the local Basque culture; all up, a spicy harvest festival. More than 20,000 tourists invade this tiny village and its 1600 inhabitants over two days. Traditional and unmistakably Basque, white Labourd houses with their low roofs, stone lintels and red or green trim line the cobblestoned streets of the commercial side of the town. However, during the festival, they are hidden amid a profusion of stalls selling chilli peppers, Salies-de-Béarn salt, Bayonne ham, *saucisson sec*, souvenirs and more. Chestnut roasters, pizza carts, street theatre and makeshift wine bars add to the jollity.

On the Sunday, I dragged everyone up early to ensure a seat at the sixteenth-century Église Saint Etienne for a celebratory mass of thanksgiving. The spectacle of all the artisan association officials dressed in their finery was much the same as at the Fête du Sel (Salt Festival). Alas, despite being over an hour and a half early, the queue continued to grow to such massive proportions that a live videocast had to be hastily arranged so that everyone could join in!

Outside this amazing fortress-like church, with its buttresses and imposing square bell tower – built in 1627 and still in working order – we stood packed like sardines with locals and tourists as we awaited the opening of the undersized side door – people were much shorter in the seventeenth century! After an hour and on the stroke of 9.30 a.m., from a house right where we were standing, out toddled a petite Madame, surely of some four-score and more years, with an iron key the size of a garden spade. To rousing applause, she made her way through the packed crowd, up the one-person-wide stairs to the crusty oak door, only to find she had the wrong key. With whoops of '*sacré bleu*' from the now anxious crowd, Madame, with the customary '*pfft*' and shrug of the shoulders, in no particular hurry, toddled back home to locate the right key and then back again. Door open, the crowd surged into the church, which features spectacular three-level, narrow wooden galleries. The seating was added after building was completed, as the congregation had grown; no town planning back then either!

The service in Occitan, punctuated with Banda music and laughter at the priests' unexpected jokes, was a jovial occasion. The artisans in their regalia ended the blessing, marching outside to the sound of jolly Basque music, through the cemetery with its

old, typically Basque disc-shaped headstones, down the valley, across the bridge. The congregation, now a rowdy crowd, followed, clapping to the beat, up to the fête-packed streets to the restored 1000-year-old castle for the annual village awards for sport, culture and, of course, chilli pepper growing. It was a delightful weekend of local celebrations.

Winter fruit and vegetables began slipping back onto the vegetable stands at the Vic-en-Bigorre market. Ali and his crew were now clad in jackets and fingerless gloves to ward off the chill. Gone were the packing cases of summer fruits, whose season had seemed to go on for many months; in their place were bins of pears and apples. To my delight, I was again able to buy basketfuls of the yellowy pale-green, flatter-shaped Chantecler apples. Our Mayor, Madame Vignaux, who also delighted at the arrival of this apple, prepared for me her family's most sensational tarte Tatin. With the apples cooked in oodles of caramelised butter and sugar under a crisp short pastry, it was without doubt the best I had ever eaten. No wonder the French love that dessert.

Turnips and swedes – *petits* for roasting and caramelising, or large for dicing up for winter potage – made their appearance along with cheeky, tightly furled little Brussels sprouts. Celery, which you can buy by the single stem if that's all you need, and endive with their chartreuse-green-edged, snow-white leaves were piled high, and there were bundles and bundles of thyme to season the Tarbais bean and confit of duck. Summer herbs were relegated to memory.

Sweet, pretty *clémentines* (a cross between an orange and a mandarin), leafy stems still intact, delighted Olive-Rose. Moist dried Agen prunes, which Jean-Luc devoured, now filled the spot where only a month ago the fresh ones shone. The children, with only a little guidance, would pick the week's fruit and vegetable requirements for me, much to the delight of Ali and his customers, who always took time to chat to them in French. Ali's was the first stand we stopped at every weekend, and the kids had a ball looking, inspecting and selecting. I wonder whether, instead of our 'don't touch' attitude in New Zealand, it was more like this, where you can pick and choose, would children be more interested in what they eat?

The crêpe maker, who had only recently set up his kitchen on wheels, was doing a roaring trade, selling crêpes by the dozen; at two euros for 12, they were a bargain. The most popular way to eat them here is lavishly spread with Nutella, something my kids screw their noses up at, just as I tell them the locals would with our breakfast toast and Promite.

Outside the *halle* (covered market), where general household goods are situated, winter boots had replaced summer sandals; coats and jackets had taken over from sunfrocks and skirts. The haberdashery seller had added wool to his stand, which was a potpourri of ribbons, buttons, zips, bias binding and sundry other knick-knacks for handicrafts. The beret seller had added scarves and balaclavas, an omen of what the next months have in store. The mobile hardware van carries everything from brooms like Harry Potter's Nimbus 2000, through dustbins, nails, hammers and other equipment to electrical and rechargeable tools. It also features a diverse assortment of mouse and rat traps for every possible location. The previous year I had freaked at these mini intruders; this year, as they came inside to find warmth and food, we took their arrival with a '*pfft*' and a shrug and moved on.

My veggie garden, once vibrant but now damp and grey, had become a mini mountain of trimmings and clippings. On a dry day I would burn the trimmings, creating a potash mix that can be dug in before winter frost and snow arrive. The fruit trees at Au Palouque had what our family calls a Max Gofton trim – my dad hacked, never pruned – and so the trees looked very bare but next year when we are not there they will fruit well, I hope.

Schooling continued with the children well and very happy. Jean-Luc was now speaking fluent French, although learning the more formal side of grammar was an on-going process. Olive-Rose spoke little French but certainly understood what was being said. My two city-slicker kids were flourishing. The days of holding onto banisters or hiding under tables to avoid going to school were long forgotten, as they scampered off early to meet friends in the *garderie* for play before school started. Farewells at school were now a mere 'see ya later Mum' and often finished with 'can you pick me up late, I want to play'. While not always best friends – it's the brother–sister thing – most days the kids were totally happy to be here. Our adventure had, we decided, been worthwhile and next month would mark our one-year anniversary; I could not believe the time had gone so fast.

PREVIOUS PAGE: Clementines – sweet,
juicy and delicious.

THESE PAGES, CLOCKWISE FROM TOP LEFT:
Picking Tarbais beans with the locals;
clouds gather over the Échez river at
Vic-en-Bigorre; cool morning light over
farmland at Labatut-Rivière; autumn
colours coat a house at the village of
Montaner; a nearby rural farmhouse;
market day at Marciac, Gers.

Piment d'Espelette

Piment d'Espelette (*Capsicum annuum*) has been cultivated in and around the Basque area since 1650. Local legend puts its arrival from South America down to a native inhabitant who crewed with Christopher Columbus on his trips to the New World. As was so often the case with many new spices centuries ago, the rare and expensive chilli pepper was used for medicinal purposes, but in time it became more readily available and locals began to cook with it, using it as a condiment and for preserving meat.

 Piment d'Espelette, one of a handful of spices with an AOC (see page 224), can be grown in only 10 communes in and around the Espelette township. Its popularity is such that today it is the foundation ingredient in Basque cookery. Production is moving with the times. In good summers the harvested peppers are strung together and hung on the sunny side of houses; the local white Basque country villas turn into a patchwork quilt of red as the peppers darken from vibrant and shiny orange-red to an intense ruby. Once dried, the peppers are tailed and dried in warm ovens for 48 hours before being ground and packaged for sale. Other businesses, taking no risks with nature, dry the peppers on open wire racks in hothouses. Once only sold whole, fresh or dried and threaded into festoons, or ground to a powder, today *piment d'Espelette* products abound, with everything from jellies to pastes, jams, pickles, seasoned salts and more.

Gâteau à la Broche

The chequered-cloth-covered table in the dining room of MOF chef Gérard Bor looks out directly to the Pic du Midi. I had been invited to share in a lunch of classic Pyrénées dishes prepared by this distinguished holder of the Médaille d'Or de l'Académie Culinaire de France.

This feast of four courses began with a heavenly Tarbais bean and foie gras velouté (egg yolk and cream-enriched puréed soup), proceeding to *gésier* (gizzard) salad and *poule au pot* (a classic poached chicken meal). The finale was Gâteau à la Broche, the quintessential gâteau of the Hautes-Pyrénées. This conical cake, with its fir-tree-like spikes, is unique in that it is cooked on a *broche* – spindle – in front of an open fire.

Its history is a molten mix of fables, fairytales and guesswork, says Gérard. The first written records date to Rome in 1310 when it was made for pilgrims who were undertaking the Chemin de Saint Jacques de Compostelle (the Way of Saint James) to Santiago. The pilgrims travelled – and still do – by way of the Ariège and Gers (then called Aquitaine), introducing the gâteau to the Pyrénées. Over the centuries, it became embedded in the culinary repertoire of the southwest, due no doubt in part to its ingredients and style of cooking, as well as its long keeping qualities.

The batter for the gâteau is a whisked mixture of eggs, sugar, flour and melted, hand-churned butter, flavoured with an abundance of strong rum, sometimes tempered with orange blossom water. The resulting air-filled batter is set to rest before being poured into a trough or tray that sits beneath or beside the fire. Once it would have sat on the hearth of a farmhouse fireplace, but today it is more likely to be part of a purpose-designed woodfire stove.

A beech or chestnut spindle, coated with baking paper and attached to a spindle with a handle at one end, sits in a brace in front of the fire. Once the *broche* (spindle) has been warmed, the long cooking process begins. The handle is turned – once a job for the wife or children – while the batter is ladled along the length of the wooden spindle. The batter gradually cooks, dripping unevenly as it turns, thus creating the spikes. The dripping batter falls into the trough beneath so that not one drop goes to waste. Its truncate shape is created during the cooking process – more batter is weighted to one end. The speed at which the spindle is turned, the thickness of the batter, its distribution on the spindle and the length of time each layer is cooked all ensure that each artisan's finished Gâteau à la Broche is different.

The long cooking was once done on long winter nights and the time varies dramatically depending on the size of the gâteau – an hour for 1 kilogram to four hours for 5 or more kilograms (the biggest, for grand fêtes, is 150 kilograms). Because of its richness and the effort required, Gâteau à la Broche is mainly prepared and shared at celebratory events such as christenings, Christmas and, in particular, weddings, at which it is often referred to as the Cake of the Bride or Shepherdess.

To serve the gâteau, thin slices are shaved across the top, exposing the layers of cooked batter, like the age rings of an old kauri. Alternatively, thicker slices are cut in wedges where the rings fall to pieces; both are acceptable. The serving should be picked up in the fingers and dunked in crème anglaise to savour. My kids loved Gâteau à la Broche, which we would buy thickly sliced from the *marché* each week; it rarely made it home for custard!

L'Haricot Tarbais

One of the pleasures of French cuisine is that even the most humble of foods is treated with reverence, and one such is *l'haricot Tarbais* – the Tarbais haricot bean – named after the nearby town of Tarbes and grown around our village.

As with so many foods of this area, its history is inextricably linked with Christopher Columbus, who brought back seeds for maize, chillies and beans among other things from his voyages to the New World. Many of these eventually found natural homes in this area. There is also a link with religion: monks were able to cultivate new crops in their monastic gardens. Monsignor de Poudenx, the Bishop of Tarbes, collected the beans while travelling in Spain at the beginning of the eighteenth century, grew them and then distributed them to the peasants and encouraged them to farm them to help alleviate endemic famine conditions.

Tarbais are a climbing or pole bean, and there were ready-made poles in the form of maize stalks; thus one for two became the rule, under which one bean was planted between two maize stalks. In 1838, records show that 14,000 hectares were planted. The bean's importance in the food supply of the masses cannot be underestimated. It could be eaten fresh or dried, kept for months, was nourishing and would economically feed a family. Enthusiasm for the Tarbais bean in the southwest flourished until the 1950s, and such was its popularity that it was sold at the Tarbes market in 80-kilogram sacks.

The war changed all that. Between a move to intensive cultivation of maize and children starting school earlier, the labour-intensive crop became too much hard work for too little return. Whereas in the 1930s 10,000 hectares were recorded as being farmed, by 1980 it was only 55 hectares. In the mid-1980s a handful of farmers sought to re-establish the bean as part of mixed cropping.

By 2000 the bean's importance to this area, the *terroir* and its unique growing style was recognised and the Tarbais bean was awarded the European IGP (Protected Geographic Indication) label and the French Label Rouge (see page 224). Only a small, close co-operative of growers are producing the Tarbais bean nowadays, but their passion promises to ensure that the Tarbais bean will return to treasure status.

Tarbais beans are hard, if not impossible, to buy in New Zealand. It belongs to the very complex *Phaseolus vulgaris* bean family and, in particular, to the haricot or navy bean variety, which can be used as a substitute for recipes in this book.

Tarbais Bean and Foie Gras Velouté

It's hard to imagine how dried Tarbais beans, fundamentally hearty, could fuse so gracefully with foie gras as to produce a soup of such a sublime texture and taste, but they do. Prepared for me by retired chef de cuisine Gérard Bor, this velvet-textured soup was such a taste experience, I had to include a recipe in this book. Foie gras is hideously expensive, but you only require a small amount to flavour this soup. Lunch with Gérard and savouring this soup will remain an abiding culinary memory of my time in the Hautes-Pyrénées.

Soaking time: overnight   Prep time: 15 minutes   Cooking time: 1–1½ hours   Serves: 8

100 grams dried haricot beans
1 carrot, peeled and diced
1 leek, white part only, chopped (avoid onion; it is too forceful in this soup)
2 stalks celery, chopped
1 bouquet garni
2 litres good-quality duck or chicken stock
100–200 grams foie gras (canned will be just fine, and use the amount you can
  reasonably afford)
2 egg yolks
½–1 cup cream

Soak the haricot beans overnight in cold water. Drain well.

In a large saucepan, place the beans, vegetables, bouquet garni and stock. Bring to the boil, lower the heat to a simmer and cover. Simmer for 1 hour or until the beans are very soft. Test by eating one or two; there should be no 'bite' left in the beans at all.

Add the foie gras and purée until smooth. I prefer using a stick blender, which makes a very smooth soup. If using a food processor, pass the soup through a sieve as well. Return the soup to the saucepan and bring it back to the heat.

Beat the egg yolks with the cream – using all the cream will achieve a very rich soup; the choice is yours. When the soup is hot but not boiling, stir in the cream mixture. Do not allow the soup to boil. Season with salt and pepper – white only, of course.

Gérard served the velouté with only croutons as a garnish. A slice of foie gras on top, although rather decadent, would be nice; I'll leave garnishing up to you.

Cèpe Carbonara

The gentle mushroom flavour of fresh *cèpes* is best served with only a few equally subtle partners. I paired the bulbous treasures that I handpicked with Monsieur Vignaux with a classic carbonara; the only other additions were garlic and parsley. My fellow mushroom *chasseur* (hunter) told me that the three make a holy trinity that can never be broken, although a little finely chopped shallot would be a nice addition.

Prep time: 15 minutes   Cooking time: 15–20 minutes   Serves: 4

6–8 rashers streaky bacon (if using smoked bacon, ensure it's mildly smoked)
1 small clove garlic, crushed, peeled and mashed to a paste with a little salt
50 grams butter
2 large fresh *cèpes* or 350–500 grams large flat mushrooms, sliced thickly
fettuccine-style egg pasta for four, fresh or dried (spaghetti would be fine)
4–5 egg yolks (freeze the egg whites for later use)
¾ cup cream or crème fraîche (not lite)
½ cup grated cheese (we used Brebis, but Parmesan is also ideal)

Bring a large stockpot of salted water to the boil. It needs to be ready to cook the pasta at the right moment.

Cut the bacon into small slices and pan-fry with the garlic and half the butter in a large, wide and preferably deep frying-pan until the bacon has well and truly softened. Set aside.

Add the *cèpes*, or whichever mushrooms you are using, and the remaining butter to the pan and cook over a gentle heat until they have softened and browned a little, or until they reach your preference for doneness. Large *cèpes* can turn quite gloopy once well cooked; I prefer them just cooked so that their slices stay whole. Keep warm.

Plunge the pasta into the boiling water – fresh will take 5 minutes, dried 10–12 minutes.

Mix the egg yolks, cream or crème fraîche and cheese together and season generously with ground pepper.

Strain the cooked pasta, leaving about ¼ cup of cooking water in with the pasta. Toss into the frying-pan along with the bacon and stir through the cream and egg mixture. Mix gently by lifting and folding over a moderate heat so that the egg sauce thickens without scrambling, coating the ribbons of pasta, and you do not break up the pasta too much. Depending on the bacon's level of saltiness, you may wish to season with a little more salt.

Fresh parsley is essential to add if you wish to have the holy trinity as Monsieur Vignaux insists, although chopped chives would make a fresh-tasting variation. Serve in warm bowls.

Slow-baked Pork with Olives

With Gascony's love of farmhouse cuisine – ducks, geese, beans and lentils – pork was never far from our menu and it was delicious. Mostly I bought pork on the bone; it was rarely available boned and rolled. As any French housewife here would tell you, the bones are essential for flavour and for keeping the roast in shape when cooking. Meat on the bone may be trickier to carve, but as my kids found out, the bones are great to chew on when carving is complete. Juicy, well-flavoured olives are essential as they will impart a delicious olive flavour to the sauce; heavily brined or hard, cheap olives will make the sauce bitter.

Prep time: 15 minutes   Cooking time: 3–3½ hours   Serves: 6

1.25–1.5 kilogram piece pork on the bone (my preference is shoulder, followed by leg; you need a cut with fat marbled through the meat)
3 stalks celery, chopped
1 onion, peeled and finely chopped
4–6 cloves garlic, crushed, peeled and thickly sliced
1 red capsicum, diced
1 not-too-hot, long red chilli pepper, sliced (deseed if wished)
½ cup of your favourite pizza or Italian-style tomato-based sauce
1½ cups chicken stock (a stock cube and water will be fine)
1 cup juicy black olives

Preheat the oven to 160°C.

Brown the pork meat well, adding a dash of oil if need be. Sit the pork in an ovenproof dish that holds the meat snugly.

Heat a frying-pan and toss in the celery, onion, garlic, capsicum and chilli pepper, and add a dash of oil if required. Stir in the sauce, stock and olives. When it's hot, pour around the pork. Cover with foil.

Bake in the preheated oven for 2 hours. Remove the foil and continue to cook for a further 45–60 minutes or until the meat is well cooked but not dry. If the sauce becomes too thick, add a little water.

Rest the meat for a good 15 minutes before carving. This is an essential step, allowing the meat fibres to totally absorb the juices. If this step is omitted, when carved the juices fall away freely. If this happens, it is an indication that the meat needs a further few minutes to rest. Mashed potatoes are a natural accompaniment.

Jambon-wrapped Cod on Potato and Pea 'Risotto'

Fresh cod, called *callibaud* here, was my children's favourite fish while in Caixon, and luckily it was to be found fresh at the larger village markets. I wrapped the cod in *jambon* and served it atop a fennel-scented potato 'risotto', for a simple, flavour-packed meal.

Prep time: 15 minutes   Cooking time: 25 minutes   Serves: 4

4 x 150 gram fillets medium-textured fish
4 long thin slices *jambon* (prosciutto is an easier-to-find alternative)

Potato and Pea 'Risotto'
500–650 grams potatoes, peeled (waxy or starchy)
½ large bulb fennel, finely diced (keep any fronds for garnish)
2 shallots, peeled and finely diced (or use a leek or white onion)
1 small clove garlic, crushed, peeled and mashed to a paste with a pinch of salt
2 cups water or mild fish stock (a stock cube and water will be fine)
1 cup frozen peas
2–3 tablespoons pastis (anise-flavoured liqueur)
½ cup cream
1 egg yolk

Preheat the oven to 160°C.

Wrap each fillet of fish in a slice of *jambon* and secure with a toothpick – it's optional, but it will help the *jambon* stay in place; just don't forget to remove the toothpick before serving. Cover and refrigerate while preparing the Potato and Pea 'Risotto'.

Dice the potatoes into small (about 1–1.5 cm), even cubes; the more even you can make the dice, the nicer the dish will look. Cook the fennel, shallot and garlic in a good splash of olive oil in a large frying-pan, only until the vegetables have wilted.

Add the potatoes and water or fish stock, cover and simmer for 15 minutes or until the potatoes are tender. Starchy potatoes are likely to fall to pieces a little; don't panic – it will add rustic charm to the finished dish. Add the frozen peas and cook for only 2 minutes, then set to the back of the stove to keep warm while you get the fish underway.

To a separate ovenproof frying-pan add a generous slice of butter, and when sizzling add the fish and brown evenly on both sides. Transfer to the preheated oven for around 6–8 minutes; the time will depend on the thickness of the fish. Return the pan to the heat, carefully add the pastis and, if you like, flambé. Turn off the heat.

Beat the cream and egg yolk together, stir into the potatoes and warm through to ensure the peas and potatoes are hot. Serve the fish on top of the Potato and Pea 'Risotto' and drizzle any pan juices over.

Madame Vignaux's Tarte Tatin

It was a privilege for us to have been made so welcome in Caixon by the Mayor Madame Elisabeth Vignaux and her family. Mme Vignaux and I would swap food and recipes and this is, without doubt, the finest tarte Tatin I have ever enjoyed. I made it with the Chantecler apple, which would soak up and hold the sensuous caramelised butter and sugar, with my second choice being Golden Delicious. Like most women here, Mme Vignaux bought her pastry, a basic short pastry, not sweetened or scented with savoury flavours. The recipe below is as given to me by Mme Vignaux, and I found I used only eight apples, but that will vary depending on the frying-pan and the size of the fruit.

Prep time: 20 minutes   Cooking time: 1¼ hours   Serves: 6 but it should serve 8!

8–10 apples
150–200 grams sugar (brown or white; I prefer white)
150 grams butter (preferably unsalted)
250–300 grams short pastry (home-made or bought; either is fine)

Preheat the oven to 180°C.

Peel the apples, quarter and remove the core.

Heat the sugar in a 27–28 cm (measurement taken from base of pan) ovenproof frying-pan over an even, moderate heat until the sugar has melted and begun to turn a light caramel brown. If you are slightly nervous about this, add a dash or two of water to help the sugar dissolve. What you do not want is for the sugar to seize and turn into a fudge-like consistency. If this happens, you will need to start again.

Add the butter to the light-brown caramel and stir to melt. Sit the apple quarters into the caramel, close together and cut side up; they will need to be packed together firmly. Place in the preheated oven and cook for 30 minutes.

While the apples are cooking, roll out the pastry to form an even circle that is 1 cm bigger than the top of the frying-pan you are using (frying-pans usually have slanting sides).

Once the apples have had their 30 minutes, carefully remove from the oven, roll the pastry on top, tuck the edges in and return it to the oven. Bake for a further 30 minutes.

Once cooked, remove from the oven and leave to stand for 5–8 minutes to allow the caramel to set somewhat. Place a large plate on top of the tart and carefully invert. Serve warm with lashings of cream – it is the absolute best.

Gâteau Basque

As the name suggests, this gâteau hails from the Basque country and it is consistently served as part of the set *plat du jour* menu at restaurants, local fêtes, and any other large gathering where food is served. Make the Crème Pâtissière ahead of time, so that it can cool.

Prep time: 1 hour   Cooking time: 45 minutes   Serves: 8–10

Crème Pâtissière
2 cups milk
½ cup caster sugar
¼ cup flour
6 egg yolks
seeds from one vanilla pod
1 teaspoon vanilla essence or extract

Pastry
2 cups flour
¼ teaspoon baking powder
125 grams butter (unsalted will make a delightful pastry)
1 egg
1 egg yolk
¾ cup caster sugar
beaten egg to glaze (optional)

For the Crème Pâtissière, heat the milk to scalding point. Work the sugar, flour, egg yolks and vanillas together in a jug or bowl to make a thick paste. Gradually stir in about ½ cup of the hot milk and, when smooth, stir this into the saucepan of hot milk. Use a whisk to stir while cooking over a moderate heat until the Crème Pâtissière is thick. Set aside, covered with a buttered piece of baking paper – buttered side down – to cool. At this point the Crème Pâtissière can be refrigerated for 2–3 days.

For the pastry, sift the flour together with the baking powder. Blend the butter, egg and egg yolk together. Work in the sugar and sifted ingredients. Turn out, bring together and refrigerate for 30 minutes or until firm enough to roll out.

Preheat the oven to 190°C and set the oven rack just below the centre.

Divide the pastry in two, with one piece just a little bigger than the other. Roll out the larger piece and use to line the base and sides of a 23 cm loose-bottomed flan tin.

The filling thickness in the Basque tarts we bought locally was usually the same thickness as the pastry, so for this thickness use half the Crème Pâtissière; or if, like me, you prefer a thick layer of Crème Pâtissière, use all of it. Roll out the remaining piece of pastry, just large enough to cover the top. Press the edges together. Brush with egg wash to glaze, if wished. Drag the tines of a fork on top to make three or four light stripes – this is the classic decoration.

Bake in the preheated oven for 35–45 minutes. It should be nice and golden. Cool in the tin for at least 30 minutes before turning out.

✻

novembre

✻

The sap had well and truly stopped rising
in the many plane, oak and chestnut trees
that grew nearby. Their leaves were falling in
bunches with every gust of wind, carpeting
our front lawn in a patchwork of autumnal
colours from crimson red to straw yellow.

LA TOUSSAINT (ALL SAINTS' DAY), 1 November, is a public holiday in France and the following day, Le Jour des Morts (All Souls' Day), is an important day for remembering past generations. In the preceding days, the shops and *marchés* in Vic-en-Bigorre and Maubourguet were a flurry of activity and colour as florist vans flooded in, packed to the gunnels with chrysanthemums in every conceivable shade. Chrysanthemums represent death in some European countries and are never given other than at a time of bereavement. Families gather for the traditional meal of *poule au pot*, before paying their respects at the graveside to family and friends, clearing away last year's dehydrated blooms and replacing them; respectful remembrance with both solemnity and smiles.

As autumn colours were now painting their way across the Bigorre Valley, with satellite navigation at hand we explored a labyrinth of tractor- and weather-worn laneways through the Baronnies, an area nestled in the eastern Hautes-Pyrénées that we had not seen hitherto.

Tucked into folds, hidden from view unless you take an unmarked turn, are tiny isolated hamlets with as few as a hundred people. Even on a blue-sky day with no grey snow clouds, limestone houses with moss-covered *lauze* (flagstone) roofs and unique stepped edges looked lonely, flowers and weeds sprouting from cracked corners and crevices.

One such village, Bourg-de-Bigorre, seemingly built for function rather than ornament, was still trying to put its roadworks, broken *fosses* (ditches) and damaged houses back together after last year's unseasonable snow and rain storms. It hosted a celebration of the *châtaigne* (chestnut), the wild version of which was once the staple of the poor. Nowadays the cultivated larger *marron* has become a luxury food for the well-off. What the festival lacked in the public relations panache of October's *piment d'Espelette fête*, it made up for in rustic charm, abounding with local character. Travellers and their children roasted chestnuts, orchardists outlined recent industry developments, weavers trimmed flax and wove traditional baskets and potters moulded clay.

Spinning the arm of the Gâteau à la Broche wheel was Georges, a wiry old chap, a magnet for the crowd. At well over 80, he sat for ages spinning cake and yarns to Jean-Luc, who had cast a keen eye over the old man's hand-carved, on-display-only hiking stick, whittled and polished from old chestnut tree branches and finished with a wild boar's tusk. Whether it was Jean-Luc's dogged perseverance, exhaustion from his nagging or a

fleeting friendship between old and young, at the end of the day Georges sold his stick to Jean-Luc; a great memento.

As always, lunch was the obligatory two-hour, four-course affair, featuring chestnuts in every course. Chunky pieces of chestnut took the place of haricot beans in the vegetable potage; chestnut flour featured in the bread – delicious but dense; caramelised whole chestnuts accompanied the lamb; and sweetened chestnut purée was blended with eggs and chocolate to make a rich sweet gâteau. Of course it was all washed down with a demi-litre of local gutsy *vin ordinaire* . . . rustic, yes; downright good, definitely.

Nearby, hidden from view, is Labastide, a wilting hamlet that seems to be home to only a handful of people and a flock of cackling turkeys. It stands out because here are caves dating back to the Palaeolithic Age. Discovered in 1938, they have only been open to visitors since 2000, although engravings and painted animals preserved for centuries on underground stone walls are out of sight in order to protect them. A video presentation of these mysteries, beamed onto the walls of the Grotte Blanche, amazes all – if only the horses could talk, what could they tell us? My palaeontologist, Jean-Luc, was in awe of this prehistoric gem and we lost him with the guide, who instructed his keen student on how to start a fire with flint and dry grass . . . oh, heavens! The kids stayed on to have fun spearing hay-stuffed lookalike animals and finger-painting with natural pigmented paints. History has never been so enjoyable.

Beyond the realms of religion, four lords ruled over the Baronnies, each with his own corner. Once a year, so the history books say, they would meet for a drink, each with one foot on their own land and the other on a neighbour's. I'm not sure what happened – whether they shuffled a two-step – but I love the yarn! They held out here for generations, surviving on the land and farming sheep in the cliff-rimmed valley. But as in so many small, beautiful but isolated valleys in the Hautes-Pyrénées, the ways of the past cannot keep up with modern farming, and the oldies have watched many young drift away.

I viewed these slowly declining villages and the isolated, ruggedly handsome Baronnies countryside from the parapets of the restored twelfth-century Mauvezin Castle, and I could visualise it as a thriving place in times past with many smallholdings, busy people, noisy animals, fires burning, travellers passing.

A year on I understand why the people of the area were – and to a degree still are – so very hardy and diffident. The geography of the Hautes-Pyrénées is such that many villages were in isolated valleys, living almost in a world of their own, self-sufficient in both sustenance and community. Over the centuries, this lifestyle has created a bounty of local customs that bring such charm to the area. Many of the customs – like saints' or village days and harvest fêtes – are still followed, and I only hope that with diminishing communities these colourful and character-filled celebrations continue; so much would be lost if they do not.

As one would expect where there is a rich history, one continually comes across intriguing tales. When I was in search of the story of Armagnac, I learned that Gascony, once called Armagnac (oh! the vagaries of French wars, revolutions and politics), was the homeland of Charles de Batz-Castelmore, Comte d'Artagnan, a heroic captain in Louis XIV's Musketeers in the seventeenth century. He was fictionalised in Alexandre Dumas' *The Three Musketeers*, published in 1844. Nowadays, the d'Artagnan of the book and numerous films is much better known than the man on whose character he was based, which is a pity because Charles had a very adventurous career before he died in battle. He took the name d'Artagnan from the family of his aristocrat mother, who was born and lived in a village next door to Caixon!

Of the many cultures and respective traditions integrated when the Midi-Pyrénées was established in the 1970s during France's regionalisation process, one uniting tradition is rugby, which here, as in New Zealand, is almost a religion. With tickets to the Stade de France to watch the All Blacks play Les Bleus, Jean-Luc and I, leaving father and daughter behind with the television, took the seven-hour train trip to Paris, along with every Les Bleus fanatic that the train could seat! Much alcohol-fuelled merriment ensured that Jean-Luc and I copped plenty of ribbing on the way up. On the way home the next day, it was a different story and we were in payback mode! We got off at Tarbes, having swapped caps, T-shirts, flags and been shouted coffee, beer and wine all the way home. The All Blacks are held in almost religious reverence here, which is hard to grasp from the other side of the world. If I had had one euro for each time I struck up a conversation with '*ma famille est de la Nouvelle-Zélande, um . . . les* All Blacks (miming haka), Jonah Lomu . . .' I could have paid for my airfare twice over! Simply put, the All Blacks open doors here to friendships – and free beer!

The Fête de la Saint Martin is celebrated at Vic-en-Bigorre. The saint has special significance in France, more so since the signing of the Armistice for the First World War on his birth date, 11 November. Roads close for the week-long fête, allowing the amusement rides and sideshow alley booths to take over. With Warwick back in New Zealand for work, the kids and I biked over after school to drive erratic dodgem cars, take pot-shots at moving ducks, picking up cheap prizes – some things are the same the world over – and sweet-talk our way through mouthfuls of *barbe à papa* (candyfloss). Despite the cold, the villagers all came out at night to party, and I wondered how much longer these traditional village fêtes would continue, in the face of growing reliance in the twenty-first century on electronic amusements, when faced with frosty autumn nights. I hope that they'll survive for some time to come, because it was great fun.

The new season's wine launch weekend had arrived again; had it really been a year? Once again I joined Francophile Brit Nick and local Joel to scout the latest releases around the vineyards. Being now considerably more *au fait* with Madiran wine, we imbibed some very fine tastings; but the lunch of truly regional fare at a local *auberge* (inn) was the highlight of the day. It was as if we had stepped into someone's oversized dining room where threadbare red and white cloths covered tables, each of which was set with basic cutlery and baskets of locally baked bread. The *potage* of Tarbais bean and winter

PAGE 300: *Escaladieu Abbey, Hautes-Pyrénées.*

PAGE 302, CLOCKWISE FROM TOP LEFT: *Freshly bottled* marrons *for sale; local gent weaving a* panier *(basket), a dying art; a* panier *full of the new season's chestnuts; Georges and Jean-Luc with his new hiking stick.*

THIS PAGE, CLOCKWISE FROM TOP: *Château de Montaner stands proudly overlooking the Bigorre Valley; the plane trees, which feature predominantly on the roads here, begin to face autumn; Warwick, Irene and I ready for action with d'Artagnan and his three trusty musketeers.*

vegetables arrived in a large crock, from which you ladled out a dish for yourself. A platter of cured meats with gherkins and a shredded lettuce and *gésier* salad followed. The entrée was a hearty *Boeuf en daube* (beef casserole), while the main course was boiled – not roasted – *confit de canard* (duck confit) and *frites* (chips). Brebis cheese and cherry jam preceded a dessert of Gâteau Basque. The bill of fare, 11 euros per person, included the *vin rouge*! I admired the simplicity of everything. At home, such straightforward food and service would fold under the expectations our world now has of food – where family-oriented fare is considered dowdy against the latest trendy fare, regardless of the fact that the latter may be far more costly, far less healthy.

At Au Palouque, the seams were bursting. I am not sure if the French have words to differentiate house from home, but after a year our *maison* was certainly the latter. Shelves groaned under a heterogeneous collection of plates, pots and jugs; drawers bulged with purchases I couldn't resist; monogrammed old linen and canteen-loads of delightful French cutlery spilled out of and piled up in every hidey-hole I could find. With this book almost completed, I would gradually pack these props ready for shipping home. I would only tackle the kids' room when I really had to, since it had become an obstacle course of two-euro purchases from the *vide-greniers* – read dust-collecting junk. The fun would start when I limited what could be taken home. Warwick's biking wardrobe was now a miscellaneous collection of every Tour de France team uniform. However, at last he had ticked off his big ambition to ride the Col du Tourmalet, the highest road in the Hautes-Pyrénées (2115 metres). He tackled what is one of the most famous and arduous climbs on the Tour de France on a clear day, getting his 'passport' stamped at the top. Doubtless the obligatory photo taken to record his achievement will soon hang on a wall of our Auckland home.

Outside, the burned garden clippings had been dug into the once vibrant garden plot, now forlorn. Bark chips had been spread on Au Palouque's courtyard garden, hopefully deterring weeds. The colour- and fragrance-filled plots I so much enjoyed creating, and which in the early days of our stay helped soothe my anxiety, were now just a memory. I was not sure that other visitors, who usually come only for a week or two, would want to undertake the work that a garden requires, so I put it back as I found it, minus the weeds.

The sap had well and truly stopped rising in the many plane, oak and chestnut trees that grew nearby. Their leaves were falling in bunches with every gust of wind, carpeting our front lawn in a patchwork of autumnal colours from crimson red to straw yellow. It was the kids' task to rake them up, which took ages because, kids being kids, it was more fun to play in them! For the most part, the children had become good friends and were settled at school, although there was still the occasional cultural hiccup, as there would be anywhere.

Thus, as November came to a close, so does this book. We decided to stay on until Easter, to eke out the last weeks we could spare from the responsibilities that waited for us back home, knowing that once the adventure was over it would not be possible to come back and live as part of a community here again, and saying goodbye was too hard just then. We were ready for the worst that winter could throw at us, but we would stay on, because the upside – good friends, possibly a white Christmas, skiing and long, cold nights snuggled up with our kids by the fire – was something Warwick and I could not turn down.

Armagnac

We have the Moors to thank for Armagnac. They brought the art of distillation to Gascony, once known as Armagnac, which borders Spain, where the Moors ruled for many centuries. While the Moors used distillation to create perfumes, the wily local inhabitants took the principles and created France's oldest *eau de vie* (brandy), Armagnac, which predates Cognac by 150–300 years, depending on the reference source you use.

This fiery *digestif* has been somewhat overshadowed by Cognac, produced further north in Bordeaux and cleverly marketed by its producers coat-tailing on Bordeaux's well-established trading relationship with Britain, which at the time was out colouring the world pink.

The three AOC-designated areas that produce Armagnac – Bas-Armagnac, Armagnac-Ténarèze and Haut-Armagnac – sit in the departments of Gers (Midi-Pyrénées) and the departments of Landes and Lot-et-Garonne (Aquitaine). The *terroir* in each impacts on the grape varieties grown for Armagnac production – Ugni Blanc, Baco 22A, Colombard and Folle Blanche.

Located 80–100 kilometres inland, the vineyards are on sandy iron-rich soil. Bitterly cold wet winters, with harsh winds from the sea and the mountains, have a profound influence on the very different style of brandy produced.

Access to markets for Armagnac was difficult when trading got seriously underway in the seventeenth and eighteenth centuries. From its landlocked source the brandy had to be shipped down small winding rivers to Bayonne, where it was transferred to ships of the Dutch mercantile marine, which were fitted out with large barrels for *brandewijn* (Dutch for 'burnt wine' – which the French call *vin brûlé* – from which the name brandy originates). As the Dutch had fewer international trading partners than the British, the market for Armagnac was correspondingly restricted.

While production of Cognac was soon consolidated under a few large-scale operators producing a relatively uniform product year after year, Armagnac has remained proudly owned by families or small businesses using the same traditional production methods as their forefathers to create a unique liquor. Nowadays Armagnac punches above its weight. It is to Cognac what the singular Spanish Almacenista Sherry is to Bristol Cream, or what aged single malt is to blended whiskies. With a number of fine producers, we were spoilt for choice of Armagnacs of differing characters and flavours.

I was fortunate to tour the oldest distillery in Gascony, Domaine d'Ognoas, dating from the thirteenth century, which is now government-owned but operating on a commercial basis to preserve its heritage and history.

In the early 1800s, the then owners, who had refined the distilling process, built a magnificent wood-fired copper alembic, or still, that is the oldest working still in the

area. The last owner, who had no heirs, bequeathed the property to the church in 1847 and in 1905 a law transferred church property to state ownership. There are a number of Domaines in Armagnac, and they play a vital and integral part in the rural economy here.

The distillation process begins in November each year. Not all vineyards have a still; they are served by roving distillers. At Domaine d'Ognoas, the historical alembic, now classified as a historic monument, is dusted off and fired up. Hefty slow-burning oak logs keep the fire burning 24 hours a day until all the season's wine has been distilled. Heat is critical to the final taste – too hot and the finished *eau de vie* will taste harsh; too cool and it will be uneven.

Each wine variety undergoes a double-pass, continuous distillation. The resulting *eau de vie*, with more than 52 per cent alcohol content, is fiery, youthful and colourless, emitting aromas of pears and prunes, violets and lime blossom. Initial ageing occurs in new oak barrels. For the Armagnac pedant, barrels should be coopered from black Monlezun oak, which imparts colour and flavour. The staves should preferably be from 100-year-old trees and seasoned in the open air for 15 years. However, the availability of these oaks is now limited and increasingly other varieties are used.

At Domaine d'Ognoas the new brandy will sleep on a while in earthen-floored cellars, as the vagaries of the four seasons are required to age it. The old fern-patterned brick walls of the cellar and the barrels inside are caked in a sooty black fungus produced from the evaporating alcohol; called the angels' share, mixing with the air, its thickness is an indicator of the quality of the brandy within. The black fungus is also visible on houses around the area, and I am told that the locals call it their 'bank', since where there is fungus, there will also be Armagnac stored away!

When the cellar master deems the brandies to have aged sufficiently he will begin the *coupage* or blending, the final critical step. The brandies will be blended – varietals from one year for a vintage Armagnac or from many years for a non-vintage. They will be sniffed, sipped and savoured until the percentages of each are agreed. Once blended, the liquor is aged further, from 10 to 40 years. If any is retained for 50 years, it will be transferred to glass *dames-jeannes* (demijohns) to prevent further influence from the oak.

The vintage Armagnacs are sold at 46 per cent at Domaine d'Ognoas, and I was treated to a tasting of the years of my choosing . . . a 1965 being the closest to my birth year, 1994 for our wedding and 2002 for Jean-Luc's birth. Since Olive-Rose's birth year has not yet been blended, we will have to return!

I cupped the brandy balloon before swirling each tasting to open up the Armagnac. Inhaling lightly – too deep and all you get is alcohol – I smelled plum, prunes, flowers, vanilla and, I think, tobacco. Viscous tears slid down the inside of the glass, an indicator of alcohol content. A sip yields the unmistakable warmth that brandy offers, but the smoothness that only Armagnac renders, achieved through patience and mystery, was sublime.

Cognac aficionados believe that the single distilling process for Armagnac does not produce as smooth a finish as the double distillation used to make Cognac. However, Armagnac, with its many family-owned businesses and labels, produces more individual and uniquely flavoured brandies. Further, since the area produces less brandy than Cognac producers lose to evaporation each year, it will remain a unique artisan product.

Jean-Luc Laffonta, Le Fermier

Jean-Luc Laffonta, farmer, Councillor of the Larreule Mairie, welcoming friend, is perched on a stool at Café Central's bar, halo rings from his petit espresso cup dotting the sports page of his copy of *La Dépêche* (Hautes-Pyrénées edition). He is checking the commodities market on his cell phone.

At first glance, this suave man, wearing Gucci glasses and smart street clothes, looks anything but a farmer – no beret, no gumboots or well-worn *salopettes* (dungarees). Nonetheless, Jean-Luc is an authentic local, a member of a family that has been here for generations. He epitomises the new generation of farmers, who, given the complexities of the European Union's agricultural directives, need to be as accomplished at business as at farming.

An economics teacher for 20 years, Jean-Luc's family's story is typical of this area, although he isn't. The family farm began with his grandparents, whose smallholding allowed for a 'few things'. His grandfather, a chef in Paris, was often away, leaving his wife to run their egg merchant business.

When Jean-Luc's grandfather retired, the next generation stepped up, although Jean-Luc's aunt ran the 12-hectare farm until his father returned from army service. From the 1960s to the 1980s, many farmers retired, selling their land but keeping their houses. Jean-Luc's father bought some of this land, gradually adding another 51 hectares to his holding. This enabled him to undertake the mixed farming of the time, with dairy, veal, pigs and maize. Ill health in the family in the 1980s led to the farm moving to beef cattle production as its mainstay, before the more recent move to single-cropping arable farming.

In 1992, reforms to the EU's Common Agricultural Policy (CAP) led to a shift in farming emphasis from animal husbandry to cropping, with cereals attracting the subsidies. In addition, the subsidies changed from product weight to land size – the more land, the greater the subsidies. Mountainous areas like the Pyrénées, where crops are harder to grow, attracted additional subsidies – a national concept to keep country villages alive since, without farming, villages in these remote areas would collapse. Many farmers turned to maize, but one-crop-only farming has proved unsustainable and will change again from 2015, when farmers must produce at least four different crops.

There are three farming styles now well established in France. The first comprises large industrial farms, mainly in northern France. The second encompasses sustainable farming, a middle way where farmers use as few pesticides as possible and proactively care for the environment. The third tier covers small farms, often organic, which sell from the gate – *la vente directe*.

Jean-Luc farms the middle way, growing maize, wheat, barley, rapeseed, sunflowers, potatoes, legumes – in particular Tarbais beans – and onions on his 70 hectares. His task, he says, is to do everything well. He is aided in this by the Signs of Quality – in his case the Label Rouge – which Jean-Luc maintains keeps farms alive, as food provenance is so important to the French.

Some farmers have established retail enterprises to ensure an outlet for their foods of quality, bypassing the supermarket trade. Jean-Luc is part-owner of a *carte ferme* (farmer's shop) in Tarbes, which sells a wide range of local, organic and sustainably produced foods. This, he maintains, is the way of the future for farmers in the second and third tiers.

Jean-Luc now employs a farm worker, freeing him up to direct the actual farming, manage the mountain of regulatory paperwork and be salesman and PR man. His produce graces the tables of local restaurants and markets, and each morning Jean-Luc takes orders from local restaurants, while checking the markets in order to sell his larger, cereal-based crops when the price is best – or, as has been the case, before planting.

It's not all beer and skittles or, to be French, café and croissants. Jean-Luc tells me that every day in the Hautes-Pyrénées another farmer locks his gates as they struggle with cheaper imported products, diminishing subsidies as more countries join the EU and lower supermarket prices. However, with modern technology, an eye for business and riding a worldwide upsurge of consumers demanding to know the provenance of their food, Jean-Luc and his fellow farmers are carving out a niche for success.

Lamb and Duck Cassoulet

Cassoulet remains the indisputable king of dishes of southwestern France, combining all the famed ingredients of this area in one hearty rustic dish. For a lesson in cooking this much esteemed meal, I spent a day with chef Pascale Salam at her cooking school, L'Atelier de Cuisine en Gascogne, in the ancient city of Auch. Deeply passionate about the traditional foods of this area, Pascale had me stirring Tarbais beans and a *mirepoix* of vegetables in a rich duck bouillon. Pascale browned the meat choices of the day: pork belly, salted overnight, duck confit portions (since this is Gascony), fresh pork sausages, thick slices of gutsy garlic sausage and Toulouse pork sausages, coarsely minced pork sausages seasoned with only salt and pepper, made long and fat. With the beans half cooked, in went the meats and then slices of fresh pork skin were placed on top before breadcrumbs were scattered over. The cassoulet was then baked slowly. The final tasting proved the worth of every ounce of effort. Pascale believes in 'real foods, in good things cooked the real way'; otherwise, she wonders, how can we be healthy? It is hard to make a classic cassoulet in New Zealand, so I have put a twist on the classic, using lamb and salted pork. Adding a few portions of duck confit (see page 90) will help make it more authentic.

Soaking time: overnight   Prep time: 1 hour   Cooking time: 2–2½ hours   Serves: 6

1 tablespoon flaky salt (less if using finely milled salt)
2–3 slices pork belly
500 grams dried haricot beans
6 cups good-quality chicken or light lamb stock
1 bouquet garni (see page 31)
1.2 kilograms lamb, cut into large, chunky pieces
6 duck sausages or chunky lamb sausages (optional)
100 grams duck fat (or unsalted butter or a light-flavoured oil)
2 onions, peeled and diced
4–6 cloves garlic, crushed, peeled and mashed to a paste with a little salt
2 tablespoons tomato paste
2 whole tomatoes, blanched and diced
a handful of coarse breadcrumbs (fresh or dry, either is fine)

Begin the day before. Rub the salt into the pork slices and place in a container in the refrigerator overnight. Soak the beans in plenty of cold water overnight. The next day, drain the beans, wash off the salt and dice the pork.

Preheat the oven to 150°C.

Put the beans, stock and bouquet garni into a large flameproof casserole and simmer gently for 1 hour or until the beans are almost tender. Brown all the meats well in the duck fat and set aside.

Add the onion and garlic to the residue fat and brown lightly. Stir in the tomato paste and tomatoes, scraping the bottom of the pan to loosen any sediment.

Stir the tomato and onion mixture and the meats into the casserole, arranging the pieces of meat evenly among the beans. If you have a friendly butcher, ask him for a piece of pork skin to put on top. Scatter the breadcrumbs over.

Bake in the preheated oven for 1½ hours or until the meat and beans are tender.

In past times, duck fat would have been added a little at a time through a hole cracked in the crumb crust. The fat softened the beans, gave flavour and, eventually rising to the top, covered the dish. When the cassoulet was cold, the fat set hard and preserved the food under the crust.

Aligot des Pyrénées

Aligot, basically a purée of potatoes and cheese, is the food of skiers in the southwest, and at the first snowfall it will be on the menu in every village *auberge* (inn) and ski-slope restaurant. To achieve its famed smooth, stringy and deliciously gloopy texture, line up some extra hands, since beating the cheese into the potatoes takes considerable effort. This is not a recipe for the waist-conscious.

Prep time: 10 minutes   Cooking time: 35 minutes   Serves: 6–8

1 kilogram starchy potatoes, peeled
¾ cup cream, hot
¾–1 cup milk, hot
125 grams butter
500–600 grams grated cheese (we used Brebis, but Cheddar is okay)

Cook the potatoes in boiling salted water until well done. Drain well and mash well – if you have a trendy potato ricer, here's an opportunity to get it out. Gradually beat in the hot cream, hot milk and butter and beat over a low heat for 5 minutes until the potatoes are fluffy. Gradually add the cheese in handfuls, beating well after each addition. Do this over a low heat. If it's too thick, add more milk or cream. Season with salt.

Serve with a spoon and fork. A bitter-leaf salad makes an ideal accompaniment to cut through the richness. It's great with sausages and mustard.

Ile Flottante

This timeless French dessert was on my examination paper way back when I was an apprentice, although we called it by its literal translation, Floating Island. Classically the islands are small sponges baked in charlotte moulds, sliced, sandwiched with jam, reformed, placed in a bowl and surrounded with a moat of crème anglaise. However, in Gascony, Ile Flottante took the form of *Oeufs à la Neige* – eggs in snow – softly poached mounds of meringue presented floating on a pool of crème anglaise and decorated with toffee. I had not seen or cooked either version since the 1970s but here it was on everyone's menu. It is a traditional dessert and quite glorious; it deserves to be revived. This recipe is included especially for Graham, who was a true Ile Flottante aficionado and together we decided that the quality of many *auberge* kitchens' skills rested on the smoothness of their vanilla crème anglaise and the softness of the islands it supported.

Prep time: 10 minutes   Cooking time: 45 minutes   Serves: 6

Crème anglaise
2 cups milk, preferably whole milk
½ cup cream
seeds from 1–2 vanilla pods or 2 teaspoons vanilla essence or extract
½ cup sugar
6 egg yolks (keep the egg whites for the meringues)

Meringues
1 litre milk, for poaching
4 egg whites
1 cup caster sugar

Bring the milk, cream and vanilla to scalding point in a saucepan. Mix the sugar and egg yolks together in a jug or bowl. Gradually pour a little hot milk into the egg mixture, whisking continuously. Transfer all the egg mixture back to the saucepan and whisk over a low heat until the custard thickens.

Transfer the custard to a cold bowl. Chill. Serve at room temperature.

For the meringues, pour the milk into a wide frying-pan and bring to scalding point.

In a scrupulously clean bowl, whisk the egg whites until they form stiff peaks. Whisk in half the sugar until the mixture is thick and fold in the remaining half.

Scoop up dessertspoonfuls of the meringue mixture and place carefully onto the hot milk. Poach, turning over in the milk, until the 'islands' are firm. Transfer to a plate while cooking the remaining mixture.

Serve the islands floating on a pool of crème anglaise. Decorate with crystallised violets.

Pascale's Pear and Almond Clafloutis

Cookery teacher Pascale prepared her version of this celebrated French dessert for me: pears cooked in richly scented vanilla syrup, rolled in almonds, embedded in a light cornflour batter and baked, but only until the batter was just done. It should be a little soft in the centre, making its own smooth sauce.

Prep time: 20 minutes   Cooking time: 20–35 minutes   Serves: 6

Pears
2 cups water
¾ cup sugar
seeds from 1 vanilla bean
4 pears, peeled, halved and cored

Batter
2 eggs
½ cup milk (whole milk is best)
¾ cup cream
¼ cup raw sugar (white would also be fine to use)
3 tablespoons cornflour
seeds from 1 vanilla bean or 1 teaspoon vanilla essence or extract
1 sachet vanilla sugar (if you cannot find this product, just omit it)
1 scant cup ground almonds

In a saucepan simmer the water, sugar and vanilla seeds for 5 minutes. Cut each pear half into three slices and poach gently in the syrup until tender. Lift the pears out and set aside to cool, but do not discard the syrup – this can be chilled and reused.

Preheat the oven to 180°C. Grease a 25 cm diameter shallow-sided ovenproof dish or six dishes of 1 cup capacity. Dust with a little of the ground almonds.

Whisk together the eggs, milk, cream, sugar, cornflour and vanillas to make a smooth batter.

Coat the pear slices in the remaining ground almonds.

Arrange the slices in the large dish or divide them equally among the smaller dishes. Pour the batter into the dish, or divide equally among the smaller dishes.

Bake in the preheated oven. The large dish will require 35–40 minutes; the smaller dishes around 18–20 minutes. Serve warm.

Adieu

I would like to think that others will be
inspired to discover this area of France
through food, and that those who dream of
taking a year out for a family adventure will
be encouraged through our experience to be
bold, step off the wheel and just do it.

CLOSING AU PALOUQUE'S BIG BLUE WROUGHT-IRON GATES for the last time was not easy for any of us. The first few desolate months of our stay were long buried in the myriad rich memories we had garnered since we had first thrown the gates open.

The children settled after the initial six months, finding their own ways to cope with the significant cultural change.

Olive-Rose, French-speaking village girl, brightened the days of her teacher and the girls at Caixon Maternelle with her spirited ways and can-do attitude.

Although Jean-Luc, for whom the cultural divide was much wider, missed the outdoor life, spirit and freedom of our new-world country, he will also miss all the aspects of mediaeval history commonplace in our area of the Hautes-Pyrénées with its rich tapestry of times past. With a good understanding of French under his belt, and a newfound love of books and mathematics, in time he will understand that the many vicissitudes were worthwhile.

In fact, both children gained confidence and discovered an ability to adapt, and they learned that history is exciting if you can experience it and live with it. The French school system of emphasis on the three Rs has, we feel, established good learning principles. We were so lucky that the teachers in both schools were outstanding. Warwick and I are delighted that, also thanks to the school system, they have been indoctrinated in good manners – and sitting still! Further, they have enjoyed entertaining themselves at home.

On the cold winter afternoons of the extra few months we stole over our year (the second winter was much less cruel than the first, thank goodness), we would take the children's bikes or scooters to one of the surrounding villages and let them ride free. On scooters, playing daredevils, they whooped with laughter as they navigated twisted plane-tree roots that protruded into the traffic-free lanes, autumn leaves flying in their wake. If they missed anything by being away from school and their friends, it has been more than made up for in the blossoming of a true understanding between brother and sister – most of the time – that will last them their lifetime.

Warwick fell in love with the area and found great satisfaction in simple pleasures (like riding his bike). It impressed him that people were so polite, well mannered, respectful and kind to us. Having his OE late in life allowed him to experience things on a different level than he would have had in his twenties. He appreciated the simple life and enjoyed occasional board games with the children or having a beer in the local *auberge*. He would try out his French and talk rugby with the old men of the village who, berets formed into a peak in line with Gascon tradition, gathered daily in the good weather to sit outside the reputed Resistance HQ for the area – what stories those walls could tell! The men's gnarled hands clasping pastis or Armagnac told of a lifetime of hard physical work. These salt-of-the-earth people welcomed us with beaming smiles and kind hearts.

I have long harboured a passion for food history, in particular spices and peasant cookery. I loved the simplicity of the food. I loved that the women here cook and that they cook food, not drizzled, dashed, dusted or otherwise embellished. I loved that they are happy to serve a simple legume soup or a mélange of fresh puréed vegetables, that a casserole is simple meat, carrot, onion and stock or red wine, and that they buy pudding, which is why there are *pâtisseries*.

Through friendship with retired chef Gérard Bor, Irene – my indispensable interpreter – and I had been welcomed into a world of food that is hidden behind crumbling walls in isolated hamlets, where ancient traditions survive as an integral part of everyday life. Respect for and knowledge of the past enables us to see the future more clearly. Food is the key to this, for all people need sustenance to live.

The best for me came in the last weeks before we returned home. The day of the *pèle-porc en Bigorre* – traditional pork kill of the region – encapsulated for me everything that is good about the way the people of Gascony or the Hautes-Pyrénées live, and it was an opportunity to participate in culinary history.

More than anything, I loved the wonderful old boys involved. We joined 82-year-old Roger and the village 'boys', all well into their sixties and schoolboy rugby mates, André, Henri, Yves and his grandson Florian, a trainee chef.

The slaughter and subsequent butchery took place in an ancient cobweb-festooned shed attached to a once grand *maison*, now crumbling. An antique, long-unused tractor was pushed out of the way so that old wooden doors could be set up as a workbench in a makeshift *boucherie* on which the men, in good humour, deftly butchered the 200-kilogram pig into the traditional cuts, dividing the meat by quality for *grillé* (grill), *rôti* (roast), pâté, *saucissons* (sausages) and *saucisson sec* (dried sausage). Everything remaining – lights (lungs), skin, trotters, ears and all – simmered away over a wood fire in a cast-iron *marmite* (a cooking pot with legs) for the *boudin noir* (black pudding).

Having started at dawn, we stopped for a morning tea, a *grillé* of freshly carved, tender pork steaks, cooked on a rough and ready open-fire barbecue in the cluttered courtyard by our MOF chef Gérard – such a long way from the starred restaurants of his professional life, but he was completely at home in this environment. The pork was washed down with pastis and Roger's home-made *vin blanc et rouge*.

The second session was spent mincing the meats and home-grown vegetables and herbs for the *charcuterie* (prepared pork meat dishes). Roger, clambering over unstable agricultural detritus like a man half his age, hung the finished sausages over the rafters of his aged barn so the cool Pyrénées air would waft in to dry them. In a few days they would

PAGE 324, CLOCKWISE FROM TOP: *Henri and Florian instruct me on how to prepare pork; Roger preparing the fire for our pork barbecue breakfast; Yves trims the leg, readying it for salting and drying.*
THIS PAGE, CLOCKWISE FROM TOP LEFT: *Gérard preparing the sausage mixture; local salt liberally rubbed into the leg and back fat; Florian, a teenager, working with Roger in the art of* charcuterie *in a time-honoured manner.*
PAGE 329: *My family outside Caixon's Mairie, dressed appropriately in Gascon berets.*

become *confit de porc saucisson* under a thick layer of creamy *porc gras* (lard) that had been carefully set aside at the initial cutting and subsequently minced.

Lunch of cheese, last year's *saucisson sec*, still preserved in the jar, and more pastis led into the afternoon's work of finishing off the *boudin noir*. All bits duly minced and mixed with the blood were filled into sausage skins before Roger took charge of cooking them. This truly skilled job required constant monitoring of the open fire beneath the *marmite* to avoid the skins splitting, which would happen quickly if the bouillon was too hot. As one of the two tables was cleaned, Yves and his grandson Florian undertook the final task of salting the ham. First they rubbed pepper around the bone to repel insects, before massaging coarse Bayonne salt crystals into and over the pork. Large planks of fat, seasoned like the ham, would be hung to dry after sitting in the salt for some days. The pork would become *jambon* and the dried fat would be eaten a slice at a time in the area's famed Garbure (cabbage soup; see page 30).

The children and Warwick joined us in the afternoon to meet these fine men. It was great for them to be able to speak French, to ask questions about what they were doing and take an interest in the ways of the past, to share a rugby joke, and to be farewelled with handshakes and even *bisous* – kisses – something not usually accorded to people, especially youngsters, who are not long-time friends.

The day finished with us all around the table, with pastis, *boeuf en daube*, cheese and a pavlova which I had decided was a suitable offering to acknowledge the privilege, as a female and a foreigner, to have been included in this traditional day. Unfortunately, such days are numbered and will soon be consigned to the history books, thanks to EU regulations that allow a 'tolerance' – license – for the elderly to be able to live and prepare their foods as they have done all their life. The license expires when the holder dies.

Discovering the food of the region, and how history and geography have shaped Gascony's culinary heritage, was greatly rewarding for us, both personally and professionally. Through my research, doors opened for all of us to friendships we would never otherwise have made, which gave us memories we would never have had and experiences that will help shape our children's future, hopefully opening up for them how amazing is the world we live in, wherever life takes them.

In writing about all this, I would like to think that others will be inspired to discover this area of France through food, and that those who dream of taking a year out for a family adventure will be encouraged through our experience to be bold, step off the wheel and just do it. What our family gained this year could never be taught in school, or read about in a travel or food magazine. However, do not dally. Gascony is changing; the European Union and the twenty-first century are seeing to that. Make the decision and go now: I promise you it will be the experience of a lifetime. Au revoir!

Acknowledgments

I am indebted to many amazing people for helping us on our family adventure and assisting me with my book; without them I would never have uncovered so much about the food and ways of life here in the Hautes-Pyrénées.

To Madame Elisabeth Vignaux, Maire of Caixon, her husband Maurice (clandestine *cèpe* hunter extraordinaire) and daughter Laure, a heartfelt thanks for making us feel so welcome and helping us to live like, and be like, locals. Caixon is a remarkable village and will always hold a special place in my heart. To the girls at the Caixon Maternelle, teacher Chantal, and *garderie* team, Mimi, Alexandrie and Myriam, thank you for your patience with my French and for the loving professional care and teaching that you gave Olive-Rose. I promise next time not to mess up the meal tickets so badly and not to get my *mercredi* confused with my *vendredi!*

To Monsieur Laffonta, Mayor of Larreule, thank you for keeping an eye on our son at the village school. To Jean-Luc's teachers, Marie-Paule and Matthieu Teixido, *merci beaucoup*, not just for the extra time helping Jean-Luc with French, but for getting him to write beautifully and love maths. Thanks also to the *garderie* girls Soso and Elodie; your support and kindness in those first few months was so appreciated.

Thanks to Carine Berges and her team at Saveurs des Pyrénées for coordinating interviews with some of the artisans who feature in this book.

Thank you to Father Thierry-Joseph and his parishioners at Saint Martin in Vic-en-Bigorre for their weekly warm greetings, and for giving Jean-Luc so much support and encouragement; he will remember his time as altar server in your age-old church with great fondness. Also grateful thanks to fellow parishioners and English teachers Isabelle Froment and Gérard Crozat, who welcomed me to their schools to work with their students, gave me their time to help with interpretations at meetings, and introduced me to the amazing Gérard Bor. Retired chef Gérard, now Secrétaire de l'Académie Culinaire de France, openly shared his passion and knowledge on the foods and culinary heritage of the Hautes-Pyrénées, without which my book would be minus many stories. I truly wished I had had more time to learn from you, but I will cherish the time that you gave me. I shall never forget Roger and the boys preparing the pig in the ways of the past; a real highlight of my stay.

There were many others, too: the artisans who feature in this book and their staff, thank you for sharing your lives with me. Thanks to the market stallholders of Vic-en-Bigorre, Marciac and Maubourguet who allowed me freedom to photograph them at work all year, and who put up with some seriously bad French on my part! *Merci* to the team at Café Bigourdan who, on the bleak, freezing cold Saturdays when Warwick was in New Zealand working, would look after *les enfants* while I shopped at the *marché*; you will find quietness now we have gone, no more squealing Kiwis riding those bikes! At Maubourguet, Melanie and her team at Café du Centre were never short of laughter to brighten my days or to welcome our visitors. Nick and Clara, fellow writers at Larreule, thank you for helping us settle in during those first few weeks when I was in a complete haze.

To the team at Happy Coulson (Pilgrim's Rest extraordinaire), Kate and Chris and their children Tana and India, a grand thank you for the best family times together – yoga, skiing, walks, joyous meals, building projects – we will be back to use that swimming pool and sleep in the beds we helped build – one day! To Beccie O'Shea, special guest at Coulsons', thank you for being my right-hand lady in the kitchen and helping me to cook up all these wonderful recipes and clean up those floods!

Thank you to the amazingly talented illustrator Perry Taylor, who prepared wonderful quirky paintings of Gascony, the inimitable Gascon farmer and us for my book.

A big heart-felt thanks to Ian Roberts, owner of Au Palouque, for allowing me to redesign his garden, and make his retreat our family's home for the year and a half we were here. Finding Au Palouque in amongst all the *maisons* for rent in the entire south of France was most serendipitous and truly wonderful.

Finally, thanks to three super people: Joan Gilchrist for holding my hand while writing – as I say, 'my cooking is better than my writing', but I got there and you made the challenge a happy one. I promise to learn where to put a dash and a semi-colon before I set off on my next book! To Graham and Irene Clarke, whose enthusiasm for this area and for my book project has led to an endearing friendship, thank you. Irene, your impeccable attention to map reading ensured that we found our way to extraordinary locations to meet amazing artisans (as I said . . . we did go to the best places!), and I am indebted to you for your patience and keen interest in being my interpreter *exceptionnelle* for the whole year – it was truly wonderful to have you with me all the way.

In closing, loving thanks to my husband Warwick, for this was his dream, without which nothing would ever have been achieved, and neither Jean-Luc, Olive-Rose nor I would be leaving a little of our hearts in the magnificently picturesque Hautes-Pyrénées.

Recipe Index

Conversions

1 teaspoon = 5 ml

1 tablespoon = 15 ml

4 tablespoons = ¼ cup

½ cup = 125ml

1 cup = 250 ml

4 cups = 1 litre

PENGUIN BOOKS

Published by the Penguin Group

Penguin Group (NZ), 67 Apollo Drive, Rosedale,
Auckland 0632, New Zealand (a division of Penguin New Zealand Pty Ltd)
Penguin Group (USA) Inc., 375 Hudson Street,
New York, New York 10014, USA
Penguin Group (Canada), 90 Eglinton Avenue East, Suite 700, Toronto,
Ontario, M4P 2Y3, Canada (a division of Penguin Canada Books Inc.)
Penguin Books Ltd, 80 Strand, London, WC2R 0RL, England
Penguin Ireland, 25 St Stephen's Green,
Dublin 2, Ireland (a division of Penguin Books Ltd)
Penguin Group (Australia), 707 Collins Street, Melbourne,
Victoria 3008, Australia (a division of Penguin Australia Pty Ltd)
Penguin Books India Pvt Ltd, 11, Community Centre,
Panchsheel Park, New Delhi – 110 017, India
Penguin Books (South Africa) (Pty) Ltd, Block D, Rosebank Office Park,
181 Jan Smuts Avenue, Parktown North, Gauteng 2193, South Africa
Penguin (Beijing) Ltd, 7F, Tower B, Jiaming Center, 27 East Third Ring Road North,
Chaoyang District, Beijing 100020, China

Penguin Books Ltd, Registered Offices: 80 Strand, London, WC2R 0RL, England

First published by Penguin Group (NZ), 2015
1 3 5 7 9 10 8 6 4 2

Copyright text, recipes and photographs (except front cover and
pages 227 (left) and 329) © Allyson Gofton, 2015

The right of Allyson Gofton to be identified as the author of this work in terms of
section 96 of the Copyright Act 1994 is hereby asserted.

Designed and typeset by Sarah Healey, © Penguin Group (NZ)
Front cover photograph © Rachael Hale McKenna
Photographs on pages 227 (left) and 329 © Grant Symon
Map of Caixon and other illustrations © Perry Taylor (www.perrytaylor.fr)
Additional editing by Joan Gilchrist
Prepress by Image Centre Ltd
Printed in China by C & C Offset Printing Co Ltd

ISBN 978-0-143-57112-4

A catalogue record for this book is available
from the National Library of New Zealand.

www.penguin.co.nz